REBUILD!

DISCIPLESHIP LESSONS FROM NEHEMIAH

BRYCE H. LOWRANCE

Original artwork by Gracie Lowrance

SOVEREIGN GRACE PUBLICATIONS
SHALLOTTE, NORTH CAROLINA

Rebuild: Discipleship Lessons from Nehemiah

Published by Sovereign Grace Publications
Post Office Box 1150
Shallotte, North Carolina 28459

sovgracepublications@gmail.com
https://sovgrace.net

ISBN 978-1-929635-35-1

Scripture quotations, unless otherwise noted, are from the King James Version.

Printed in the United States of America

Acknowledgments

For all those that love the Lord but find themselves poor sinners, may God bless each of us to seek His face and put His will ahead of our own.

Thank you to my dear wife, Terri, of 30 years for having the patience to let me grow-up and rebuild my life together with her. She and my daughter, Rebecca, spent countless hours proofreading this book and teaching me grammar! I am thankful for our five children who love the Lord and His church. Thank you also to Chris Edwards for your attention to detail in my daily blogs and in the editing of this work.

A special thanks to my daughter, Gracie, who designed and drew the images for these articles and the coloring book.

Why Study Such an Old Book?

We live in the 21st century and have the New Testament in our Bibles, so why would anything in the Old Testament be of beneficial study for us today?

Paul told Timothy that:

> *"All scripture is given by inspiration of God, and is profitable for doctrine, for reproof, for correction, for instruction in righteousness: That the man of God may be perfect, throughly furnished unto all good works." – 2nd Timothy 3:16-17*

At the time of Paul's writing, the New Testament saints only had the Old Testament for study. It was all they needed to walk a perfect (or complete) walk. If it was profitable for *their* Christian discipleship, it is for ours as well.

The Book of Nehemiah records a pivotal time in the history of Israel when the city of Jerusalem was partially restored to its former majesty. Ezra had coordinated the rebuilding of the Temple several years before. In this book, a fellow Jew comes to tell Nehemiah that the people who have returned to Jerusalem are being mocked because the city walls are destroyed, and the city is vulnerable. Upon hearing the news, Nehemiah weeps for Jerusalem and prays to God.

Nehemiah's prayer and dedication to the Lord are recorded as the walls are rebuilt against all odds in only 52 days! The restoration of order in the city and the additional repentance from backsliding are recorded for us too. There are amazing parallel lessons to apply to rebuilding and revitalizing a personal life, a family, or a church.

This study will look at the restoration of Israel from the perspective of rebuilding our personal, family, and church-family discipleship. The pandemic and pivotal changes in American government and ideology revealed to me and many other Christians that we may not be prepared to live like Christ in a world that is becoming more and more like Babylon. We each need to rebuild or revitalize the broken down parts of our discipleship so that we may face the struggles of not only a world that is against us, but also the difficulties of our day-to-day lives. I hope that you will join me in this adventure, and I pray that God will bless our time spent in His word. Followers of Christ at any age could benefit from daily repentance and renewal.

Format of This Devotional Book

This devotional study is designed to follow the pattern of the 52 days it took for the Israelites to rebuild the walls of Jerusalem. These brief devotionals may be used to improve discipleship as an individual, to strengthen your family, or to build up the unity of your home church (as well as other ways). You can do it as a daily devotional, or take one devotional per week for a year-long study. The study can also be read at your own speed of comprehension and application. However it is approached, the book is intended to be applied as a whole, not just small portions by preference.

I have attempted to write this little book in such a way that any person can study it alone. Smaller children may need help with some of the vocabulary, but the core of the book is written on a 6th to 8th grade reading level. There is an additional coloring book that should assist families and churches in family-integrated study of the word of God. The images at the beginning of each devotion correspond to a coloring page in that book.

Following each devotional, there are a few discussion starting questions for self-reflection and family or group discussion. These can certainly be modified to fit any setting or age group.

In particular, I hope this book will help motivate teens and young adults to focus their lives on Jesus Christ. Those years are some of the most critical in a person's life. It is at that time a person typically decides what kind of life he wants to lead. I pray this study will help you live a life devoted to God.

> *"Seek ye the LORD while he may be found, call ye upon him while he is near:"* – Isaiah 55:6

> *"Remember now thy Creator in the days of thy youth, while the evil days come not, nor the years draw nigh, when thou shalt say, I have no pleasure in them;"* – Ecclesiastes 12:1

A Little Background

To better understand what is happening in the Book of Nehemiah, let's look at a small timeline of events leading up to Chapter 1.

- Israel disobeys God (again). Jeremiah has prophesied that God will purge Israel of its sin by giving them over to captivity.
- 607 B.C. Babylonian conquest begins. Daniel is exiled. Jeremiah's 70 years begins.
- 599 B.C. Ezekiel is exiled.
- 588 B.C. More than 50,000 Jews are taken to Babylon. Lamentations is written.
- 538 B.C. Babylon is conquered by Persia. Daniel is given a position in the Persian court.
- 538 B.C. Cyrus allows Israel to begin returning to Judah.
- 515 B.C. The Temple is rebuilt as encouraged by Haggai and Zechariah.
- 472 B.C. Esther becomes queen of the Persian Empire.
- 467 B.C. Another group of exiles returns led by Ezra.
- 454 B.C. Another group returns to Jerusalem with Nehemiah and rebuilds walls.

The major characters at this time are Zerubbabel, Ezra, and Nehemiah. Zerubbabel rebuilt the temple, Ezra brought back the preaching of the word, and Nehemiah was responsible for the rebuilding of the city walls and acting as governor.

We will find that Nehemiah wears many hats in this history. He is an intercessor in going to the king of Persia. He coordinates a massive move of people, supplies, and equipment as they return to Judah. He engineers the plan to rebuild the walls. He acts as a military leader when trouble comes up. And finally, he acts as governor to restore peace and civility.

1 • God Is Not an ATM

"The words of Nehemiah the son of Hachaliah. And it came to pass in the month Chisleu, in the twentieth year, as I was in Shushan the palace," – Nehemiah 1:1

"And it came to pass in the month Nisan, in the twentieth year of Artaxerxes the king, that wine was before him: and I took up the wine, and gave it unto the king. Now I had not been beforetime sad in his presence." – Nehemiah 2:1

Before we even get into the heart of the message of Nehemiah, I would like to point out a major principle of prayer and serving the Lord. *God is not an ATM.*

We live in a microwave society where we get upset when it takes more than two minutes to get our fast-food burger. God's timing is not our timing. And sometimes we must wait a long time for an answer to prayer.

The month of Chisleu is equivalent to our November/December time frame. The month of Nisan is equivalent to our March/April. This means that Chapter 1 of this book is about four to five months in length. Nehemiah wept for

Jerusalem for four to five months. He prayed for God's help for four to five months. He waited on the Lord for four to five months!

But look at the results of his wait. God answered, and He answered **BIG TIME!**

Today's "religion" often promotes some form of prosperity doctrine that teaches you can have anything you desire if you just ask in faith. This concept is foreign to scripture. The subject and content of our prayers need to be according to God's will.

> *"And this is the confidence that we have in him, that, if we ask any thing **according to his will**, he heareth us: And if we know that he hear us, whatsoever we ask, we know that we have the petitions that we desired of him." – 1ˢᵗ John 5:14-15*

The powerful answer to Nehemiah's prayer is a wondrous blessing that has its foundation in the will of God, not the desires of Nehemiah. Nehemiah is asking for something that gives God glory and benefits the kingdom of God. Our prayers should seek these two primary motivators before we ever ask for something for ourselves.

A proper foundation for building our lives on the Jesus of the Bible is essential. One of the most important traits of a disciple of Christ is humble yet fervent prayer. We can use the model prayer found in Matthew, Chapter 6 to show us what the basic content of our prayers should be.

> *"And when thou prayest, thou shalt not be as the hypocrites are: for they love to pray standing in the synagogues and in the corners of the streets, that they may be seen of men. Verily I say unto you, They have their reward. But thou, when thou prayest, enter into thy closet, and when thou hast shut thy door, pray to thy Father which is in secret; and thy Father which seeth in secret shall reward thee openly. But when ye pray, use not vain repetitions, as the heathen do: for they think that they shall be heard for their much speaking. Be not ye therefore like unto them: for your Father knoweth what things ye have need of, before ye ask him.*

> *"After this manner therefore pray ye: Our Father which art in heaven, Hallowed be thy name. Thy kingdom come. Thy will be done in earth, as it is in heaven. Give us this day our daily bread. And forgive us our debts, as we forgive our debtors. And lead us not into temptation, but*

deliver us from evil: For thine is the kingdom, and the power, and the glory, for ever. Amen." – Matthew 6:5-13

Here are some of the main points Jesus teaches us about our prayer-life:

- Prayer is between you and God. It should not be used to be seen as more righteous than other people.
- Prayers should not be the words of others. We are to speak from a heart of faith (Hebrews 11:6).
- Prayer should acknowledge that God is the King of all creation, and yet is a loving Father. We should never address Him like we would our casual friends.
- Prayer should seek the will of God to be done on earth, especially in our own lives and needs.
- Prayer should be for a specific purpose or need, and those needs should be in accordance with scripture (1st John 5:13-15).
- Prayer should ask for a closer fellowship with God.
- Prayer should ask for direction from God in leading us to live a more righteous life for His glory.
- Prayer should acknowledge that God has all the power, and all the glory is due to Him regardless of how He answers our prayers.

One of the most important steps in rebuilding our life for Christ is proper attitude in prayer. Let us pray like Nehemiah for the glory of God in His kingdom. And even when we are asking for our personal needs, let us focus on how we can help others as God provides for us.

Build your wall...

How would you describe your current prayer life?

What kinds of things should we pray about or for?

What kind of responses should we expect from God?

2 • Voluntary Servitude

"For I was the king's cupbearer." – Nehemiah 1:11c

After Cyrus conquered Babylon, he allowed the Jews to begin returning to Jerusalem. It is not certain whether he denied anyone permission to leave on their own. Therefore, it is possible Nehemiah remained in Persia by his own will or as an act of faith.

He was the king's cupbearer, which meant he was basically part of the ancient secret service. He protected the king from poisoning by tasting his drink before serving it to him. Nehemiah had a place of great honor in Persia and great influence as well. The king had come to trust him and was close to him. Whether Nehemiah was there willingly or by force does not matter. He chose to serve as if he was serving the Lord. He was faithful to his position, and it ended up working to the benefit of all of Israel.

We may not always know why we are in our current circumstance of life, but we do know that God is with us. We should act in faith and integrity, as serving the Lord.

Contrary to the modern trend of what I call "Christian Superiority," the Bible teaches us that, to be like Jesus Christ, we must have *humility*.

> *"Let this mind be in you, which was also in Christ Jesus: who, being in the form of God, thought it not robbery to be equal with God: but made himself of no reputation, and took upon him the form of a servant, and was made in the likeness of men: and being found in fashion as a man, he humbled himself, and became obedient unto death, even the death of the cross." – Philippians 2:5-8*

We should not have the attitude that, if I follow God, He owes me something for my obedience. God owes us nothing! Neither should we think that we are better than others because we are following the Lord. We are His servants. Servants do not seek their own honor.

Nehemiah gives us the perfect example of how we can act like Christ. He served God by serving an earthly king. We should do the same by serving one another. The only way we can truly love and serve God is to humble ourselves and become servants of others.

I believe "Free-Will Doctrine" is the cause for this superiority complex that many Christians have today. This "gospel" is being used to scare people into obedience, and anyone who does not immediately follow is labeled as a "hell-bound" sinner. This leads the followers of Christ to have a superior feeling about themselves because *they chose* the right path. The true gospel brings comfort, not fear. We should follow the Lord in freedom and thankfulness because He finished our salvation in Jesus Christ.

Secondly, the gospel, or any message claiming to be the gospel, should not be used for personal gain of wealth or power. The current trend of prosperity doctrine is spreading like a cancer in churches all over America. It teaches that the clearest evidence of God's favor on you is material wealth and success. This concept is *completely* foreign to scripture. A Christian, according to the Bible, looks and acts like Jesus. Now, I am not saying that we should sell all our material blessings and become homeless, but Jesus was homeless during most of His earthly ministry and taught us not to concern ourselves with personal comforts. He taught us that God would take care of our basic needs of food and clothing.

> *"But seek ye first the kingdom of God, and his righteousness; and all these things shall be added unto you." – Matthew 6:33*

Furthermore, the Apostle Paul understood that suffering is what actually brings us closest to Christ.

> *"That I may know him, and the power of his resurrection, and the fellowship of his sufferings, being made conformable unto his death;"*
> *– Philippians 3:10*

Paul says that, to truly understand the power of the resurrection, we must suffer for righteousness' sake. Furthermore, Paul found peace in serving God in whatever position he was in. The following verses, often yanked out of context to try to prove un-Biblical principles, show us that if we live in service to Christ we will have peace and contentment, like Paul.

> *"Not that I speak in respect of want: for I have learned, in whatsoever state I am, [therewith] to be content. I know both how to be abased, and I know how to abound: every where and in all things I am instructed both to be full and to be hungry, both to abound and to suffer need. I can do all things through Christ which strengtheneth me." – Philippians 4:11-13*

God calls people from every financial station there is. Rich or poor is no better evidence of salvation than the state or country in which you live. Nehemiah's example teaches us to serve the Lord where we currently are. And, if the Lord sees fit to move us or use us in a bigger way, we should continue in prayer, seeking His guidance. We must have the mind of Christ, which is the idea of humility and voluntary servitude.

And always remember,

> *"He that is faithful in that which is least is faithful also in much:"*
> *– Luke 16:10a*

Whatever our age, education, or secular occupation may be, we should first consider ourselves as servants of the Lord. When we have a servant's attitude, our will does not matter. As we have already seen, we should be praying according to God's will. The next step is to make sure we are *living* God's will for us.

Build your wall...

✗ What does a "servant attitude" look like?

✗ Describe some Biblical examples of what children of God were called to do both pleasant and unpleasant.

✗ How do we improve our role as servants?

3 • Bad News from the Homefront

"The words of Nehemiah the son of Hachaliah. And it came to pass in the month Chisleu, in the twentieth year, as I was in Shushan the palace, That Hanani, one of my brethren, came, he and certain men of Judah; and I asked them concerning the Jews that had escaped, which were left of the captivity, and concerning Jerusalem. And they said unto me, The remnant that are left of the captivity there in the province are in great affliction and reproach: the wall of Jerusalem also is broken down, and the gates thereof are burned with fire."
– Nehemiah 1:1-3

Nehemiah was going about his daily routine as the cupbearer in the house of the king of Persia when some of his Jewish brethren, including his brother Hanani, came to him with news from their homeland. And that news was not good at all.

The Temple had been rebuilt, but the city was lying in waste. All the Jews who had returned there were mocked continually by the surrounding nations and were in horrible danger, because the city of Jerusalem had no walls of defense.

The theme of wall building is the central point of our study in the Book of Nehemiah. The spiritual lesson we must learn from this opening is that we are never truly safe in this fallen world. The Jews had been freed, but the Lord's people have enemies everywhere. They had returned to their home and tried to restart worship, but they were in continual danger of losing it all again.

We, too, have been set free by the finished work of Jesus Christ, but there is a battle that still remains. The Bible does not promise prosperity and safety in this world simply because we follow Christ. We must guard our hearts and minds against the enemies of God.

We need to see that there may be destruction lying at the door and be prepared to rebuild the parts of our lives that are vulnerable. Our salvation is secure in the Lord, but our ability to *live in* that liberty is in jeopardy if we do not stand ready to build and battle every day. As America dives deeper into depravity, we must understand that we have been blessed for over 240 years with great freedom of expression and religion. But now, Babylon is taking over. Our communities are growing more and more hostile toward God and therefore against us.

The first step in strengthening the defenses of ourselves, our families, and our churches is repentance. If we know we are doing something contrary to the will of God, we should stop immediately. Even if we haven't experienced adverse consequences because of a particular sin, we should not expect that to always be the case. Repentance from sin should be a daily focus in our Christian walk. To be like Christ, we must be less like the world!

Secondly, much like the first step, we need to be studying the word of God regularly. This will help identify more holes in our defenses and also teach how to repair the broken parts of our lives.

With these two fundamental points guiding us every day, we should then be in prayer that God would lead us in righteous paths. Then, we should listen or watch for His leading!

We will learn later that we need to keep a constant watch for enemies. Right now, we should closely examine the kinds of entertainment to which we expose ourselves. Television, movies, the Internet, and even secular books should be carefully considered before we allow them to influence us because these things will influence us more than we realize!

We are *all* being constantly educated, not just our children. Every moment of every day we are learning from what we see, read, hear and experience. Even the kind of formal education that we pursue should be compared to the word of God constantly. Remember, Babylon of old tried to change the names of God's people, feed them differently, and educate them in the ways of confusion. We need to focus on God and His word.

All these things *can* distract us from following God and not see the danger around us:

- TV, entertainment
- Secular education
- Pride
- Comfort
- ____________________?

We must also remember that when we step away from the world and toward God, we will stand out and be strangely different than the fallen world around us. We need to be ready to contend for the faith. Prayer is an important part of this but so is focusing on the word of God and removing distractions from and hindrances to our discipleship.

Build your wall...

- Do you mourn for the condition of your church/ country/ family?

- What distractions are in your life that create holes in your defense?

- How do you balance living in the 21st century and yet still battle against the evil in the world?

4 • True Repentance

"And it came to pass, when I heard these words, that I sat down and wept, and mourned certain days, and fasted, and prayed before the God of heaven, And said, I beseech thee, O Lord God of heaven, the great and terrible God, that keepeth covenant and mercy for them that love him and observe his commandments: Let thine ear now be attentive, and thine eyes open, that thou mayest hear the prayer of thy servant, which I pray before thee now, day and night, for the children of Israel thy servants, and confess the sins of the children of Israel, which we have sinned against thee: both I and my father's house have sinned. We have dealt very corruptly against thee, and have not kept the commandments, nor the statutes, nor the judgments, which thou commandedst thy servant Moses." – Nehemiah 1:4-7

For more than four months, Nehemiah mourned for the sins of Israel. In his prayer, he recognizes God for His mighty and wonderful nature. He acknowledges that Israel's sin was against *this* perfect God. He doesn't give excuses or try to explain away their behavior. He simply says, "God, you kept your end of the bargain, we did not." He offers no basis for the return of God's blessing other than the fact that God keeps His covenants. And God had promised to bless Israel again if they would repent.

Repentance from sin is so much more than just a promise we will never do something again. It comes only after there is genuine mourning for the sin we have committed. This mourning for sin is not for the fact that we got caught but the fact that we offended the Lord of Glory!

True repentance comes only when we realize that our sin is against a Holy, Righteous, All-Powerful God, Who sent His Son to die for that sin. When we truly see how offensive we have been toward the God Who loves us, then we can feel His hand of mercy blessing us with a spirit of repentance and conversion.

When that spirit of repentance does come, we must fall on our knees thanking God once again, for He alone can grant the mercy and grace necessary to break our hard hearts. Our prayers should not contain anything about what we can *claim*. For all we can claim is that we are sinners that have fallen short of the glory and righteousness of God. Our prayers *should* contain a humble plea for mercy based on the finished work of Christ alone.

Consider the words of David when confronted by the prophet Nathan after he had murdered Uriah and taken Bathsheba:

> *"Have mercy upon me, O God, according to thy lovingkindness: according unto the multitude of thy tender mercies blot out my transgressions. Wash me throughly from mine iniquity, and cleanse me from my sin. For I acknowledge my transgressions: and my sin is ever before me. Against thee, thee only, have I sinned, and done this evil in thy sight: that thou mightest be justified when thou speakest, and be clear when thou judgest." – Psalm 51:1-4*

David begged for God's mercy according to God's lovingkindness, not because he deserved it or even that he had asked. David understood that his only hope was based in the mercy of God. David also acknowledged that the true horror in his sin is not only what he had done to Uriah, but that he had sinned against the Holy God. Our sins can and do affect not only our personal lives but the lives of those around us. This can be tragic at times. However, we need to look at our sin even deeper to see that we have offended God by what we have done or are doing.

A little further into the Psalm, we see that David understands that he has been foolish and selfish. He begs for the joy of his salvation to return, and pledges that when it does, he will seek to be a blessing to others rather than focusing on his personal desires. So basically, he prays for a servant's heart!

"Restore unto me the joy of thy salvation; and uphold me with thy free spirit. Then will I teach transgressors thy ways; and sinners shall be converted unto thee." – Psalm 51:12-13

Repentance should be a regular part of our discipleship.

If we do not recognize the things we need to turn away from, we can ask God to show us, and He will! When we see those sins, we should beg God for help in turning away from them and back to Him. And we should also remember, the "little sin" that we may think is no big deal is the hole in our defenses where Satan *will* make his attack!

Build your wall...

- Describe how patience and prayer work together in our spiritual growth.

- What should our attitude be concerning "little sins"?

- Is repentance just thinking differently or is it something more? Explain.

- What do you need to repent of?

5 • By God's Mercy Alone

"Remember, I beseech thee, the word that thou commandedst thy servant Moses, saying, If ye transgress, I will scatter you abroad among the nations: But if ye turn unto me, and keep my commandments, and do them; though there were of you cast out unto the uttermost part of the heaven, yet will I gather them from thence, and will bring them unto the place that I have chosen to set my name there. Now these are thy servants and thy people, whom thou hast redeemed by thy great power, and by thy strong hand." – Nehemiah 1:8-10

In this portion of his prayer, Nehemiah gives three reasons why God should have mercy on Israel again. You will notice that *none* of them are based upon Israel's merit but upon the mercy of God.

The covenant that God made with Israel is that He would bless them if they would repent of their sin and turn back to Him. On the surface, this may seem like God owes Israel a blessing for obedience, but that is far from the truth. As we learned in our previous study, the ability to repent *only* comes from God. It is His act of mercy that breaks our hearts and allows us to mourn for our sins against Him. You will also notice that Nehemiah rightly points out that it is God alone Who will gather the people scattered all over the heavens. Grace is *not* doing our part to meet God halfway. We cannot come to Him first. We love Him because He first loved us!

The second detail, which is often overlooked, is the place where the blessing will take place. God chose Jerusalem as the place for Israel to worship Him. Israel would have chosen, and did choose, many other places to try to worship, but God had a specific location. All efforts to worship outside of God's appointed place led to further error and the withdrawal of God's providence.

It is by His sovereign choice when and where blessings will pour out on His people. In the New Testament times (which is today as well), God filled out the shadow of Mount Zion in His church (Hebrews 12:22-23). The church of the Lord Jesus Christ is now where God has sovereignly chosen to commune with His people. As it is recorded in the Book of Acts, The Lord added daily to the *church* such as should be saved (Acts 2:47). This does not mean that God cannot or does not provide blessings to us away from church, but it does mean that He has promised He *will* bless His church. If we are seeking the favor of God, the best place to be is in the fellowship of a church!

The last reason Nehemiah gives for God's blessing is that Israel is His chosen people. God had sovereignly chosen them, delivered them, and redeemed them from bondage by His mighty power. They are His people! The mercy of election makes us God's children. In Romans, Chapter 9, Paul reminds us of God's own word, "I will have mercy on whom I will have mercy, and I will have compassion on whom I will have compassion." It was His sovereign choice of us that made us sons of God, and it is His sovereign mercy that brings repentance to the hearts of His people.

Nehemiah's prayer truly is an excellent example of humility and reliance on an Omnipotent God to show everlasting mercy.

Today's lesson has given us further instruction in how we ought to live and pray. We have nothing of merit that we can claim. We must rely on God. But here is the joyful hope we have — God is the Father of Mercies. He delights in showing mercy to His children. Today, let us ask for mercy from God for our country, for our community, for our church, for our family, and for ourselves.

Build your wall...

✕ What does it mean that God is sovereign?

✕ What can you do to improve your attitude and devotion to the Lord through your local assembly?

✕ Describe to others God's acts of mercy toward you.

6 • Grant Me Mercy

"O Lord, I beseech thee, let now thine ear be attentive to the prayer of thy servant, and to the prayer of thy servants, who desire to fear thy name: and prosper, I pray thee, thy servant this day, and grant him mercy in the sight of this man. For I was the king's cupbearer."
— Nehemiah 1:11

The concluding verse of Nehemiah's prayer continues to beg for mercy from the Almighty.

God is not obligated to hear the prayers of anyone, even His own people. So, Nehemiah begs God to listen. However, there is a joy in knowing that God *does* hear our prayers and that He *delights* to bless us when we seek His help in prayer! He blesses, not out of obligation to us, but out of pure love and compassion for His children.

Nehemiah also says that Israel desires to fear God's name. He is pleading for that spirit of repentance necessary to bring about true change. It is only when we see how powerful God is, that we understand how merciful He is toward us.

Modern Christianity has far too low a view of God and His majesty. Jesus called us friends, but many Christians treat Him like they do a common friend, forgetting to speak to Him as the King He truly is!

Finally, Nehemiah asks for mercy for the job he was about to perform. Remember, he is part of the "secret service" protection squad for the king. His job as cupbearer was to prevent the king from being poisoned. He was close to the king, and he is about to look and act a lot differently than he had before. Nehemiah knew that if the king suspected anything amiss, not only could he refuse to listen to Nehemiah, but he could also have him banished from the court or killed.

We, like Nehemiah, live in the real world. Others see our actions and hear our words. We should be praying that God would, in His mercy, help us to walk as His children in all circumstances of life.

Sometimes, it is easy to be a Christian. Whenever most of those around us love the Lord, it is easy to express ourselves and be bold in the Lord. However, we live in an increasingly hostile world. Babylon hates God, therefore the world hates us. It is in these situations that we especially need the mercy of God to be strong and of a good courage. For we need to have courage to do the things God would have us to do and to live the way God would have us to live in a world that cares nothing for us and hates the God we love.

As we reflect on this entire prayer, let us notice the humility. Mark the spirit of begging that Nehemiah uses when praying to a Sovereign King. And then realize something that is absolutely awesome. God answered his prayer! Oh, what wondrous love is this!

> *What wondrous love is this, O, my soul, O my soul!*
> *What wondrous love is this, O my soul!*
> *What wondrous love is this, that caused the Lord of bliss*
> *To bear the dreadful curse for my soul, for my soul;*
> *To bear the dreadful curse for my soul!*
> *— From Dupuy's Hymns and Spiritual Songs*

Build your wall...

Do we *deserve* the grace and mercy of God? Explain.

What is the difference between fake and true humility?

Describe how you act in church compared to in the world.

7 • A Conversation with the King

"And it came to pass in the month Nisan, in the twentieth year of Artaxerxes the king, that wine was before him: and I took up the wine, and gave it unto the king. Now I had not been beforetime sad in his presence. Wherefore the king said unto me, Why is thy countenance sad, seeing thou art not sick? this is nothing else but sorrow of heart. Then I was very sore afraid, And said unto the king, Let the king live for ever: why should not my countenance be sad, when the city, the place of my fathers' sepulchres, lieth waste, and the gates thereof are consumed with fire? Then the king said unto me, For what dost thou make request? So I prayed to the God of heaven." – Nehemiah 2:1-4

After over four months of weeping, fasting, and praying, the Lord gives Nehemiah an open door to talk with Artaxerxes about rebuilding Jerusalem. During all this time, Nehemiah kept his mourning secret and composed himself as a joyful servant every day.

History tells us that, about this time, Artaxerxes has returned from a battle in Egypt. Even though he was victorious, the king was probably in no mood to have more problems brought unto him. It is on *this* occasion that Nehemiah, noticeably distressed, comes before the king. The king takes immediate notice and asks him what is wrong. Given these facts, we can understand why Nehemiah becomes "very sore afraid."

However, this is not a lack of faith on Nehemiah's part. Remember, Nehemiah is basically part of the ancient secret service. His job was to protect the king from poison by tasting his wine. If this agent, who is supposed to be protecting the king, suddenly looks depressed or nervous it would alert the king of possible danger, possibly even from Nehemiah himself. The king could banish Nehemiah or have him killed immediately! Rather than this being a moment of lapsing in faith and being afraid, it is an example of one of the purposes of faith in strengthening you with courage despite the fear. Nehemiah's faith helps him overcome the fear and speak to the king.

"Let the king live forever"

He begins his speech by showing due honor to the civil authority over him. According to Romans, Chapter 13, we are to be subject to higher powers, and, when those powers do not command us to violate the word of God, we are to show them obedience as well as proper respect.

Nehemiah then describes why he is so distressed. His homeland is a wasteland, and his fellow countrymen are mocked and in danger every day. Here is the pinnacle moment of the conversation. The king could, at worst, laugh at his calamity and have him killed. Or the king could allow Nehemiah to make a request. The latter is not likely given the position of the king, but *this* is the very moment of mercy that Nehemiah had prayed for at the end of Chapter 1.

This king's heart is in the hand of God (as all are), and the Lord grants mercy to Nehemiah. The king asks Nehemiah what he would like to do. Nehemiah had been praying about this for over four months. There is no doubt he knew exactly what he needed to do. He could have immediately listed his entire plan to the king, but he doesn't. He does something else first. Nehemiah prays. He had been praying for months, but he prays one more time. This time he prays in the presence of the king. This is the moment of truth for Nehemiah. He does not trust himself. His faith leans on God who gave it to him.

"So I prayed to the God of heaven."

The story of Nehemiah has a spiritual application to us. We need to rebuild various parts of our lives and draw closer to Christ. In this account, we learn that there will be times that we are afraid and face grave danger. That is when we need to remember our God-given faith and press on, always remembering to keep the conversation with God open through prayer.

Our lives are filled with decisions both small and great. We should take each situation to the Lord in prayer, and then…

wait.

We should wait for His answer. And then we should pray again and again as we move forward in His service. God never intended for us as individuals or collectively as family or church to sit idly during our lives. To be active in God's service takes courage. Therefore, we ought to pray for courage and then use it!

Build your wall…

- How should we act toward those in authority over us?

- How long does it take for God to answer our prayers?

- What should we do when we have prayed, but God has not answered yet?

- What does an answered prayer look like?

8 • Three Wishes

"And I said unto the king, If it please the king, and if thy servant have found favour in thy sight, that thou wouldest send me unto Judah, unto the city of my fathers' sepulchres, that I may build it. And the king said unto me, (the queen also sitting by him,) For how long shall thy journey be? and when wilt thou return? So it pleased the king to send me; and I set him a time. Moreover I said unto the king, If it please the king, let letters be given me to the governors beyond the river, that they may convey me over till I come into Judah; And a letter unto Asaph the keeper of the king's forest, that he may give me timber to make beams for the gates of the palace which appertained to the house, and for the wall of the city, and for the house that I shall enter into. And the king granted me, according to the good hand of my God upon me." – Nehemiah 2:5-8

The King has seen that Nehemiah is in distress. Nehemiah has told him why, and now the King asks what Nehemiah needs. This is the moment that courage is needed. Nehemiah could have asked for something small, but he knows that God has a large work for him to do, so he asks for it all.

Request #1

Nehemiah asks for a leave of absence to travel back to Jerusalem and rebuild the city walls. This is not simply asking for a few weekends off. It was at least a four-month trip by foot one-way! Not to mention that he would need to gather supplies, build the wall, and then return to Persia. Nehemiah 5:14 shows us that he was gone about twelve years! This is a huge request. And the king, by the mercy of God, grants the request.

Request #2

Nehemiah asks for letters granting him safe passage through all the king's territories. On the surface, this would seem like a small request, but we need to remember that Persia did not rule like Babylon. The society was more open and not under direct military control. There were many nations that hated Israel between Sisera and Jerusalem. Ezra made a similar request upon his return, and this request was answered in the same way. God's mercy abounds even more in the king's response to Nehemiah. Nehemiah not only got letters of permission to work and passage to go, he got a military escort for the trip!

Request #3

Nehemiah's final request was the most bold. He asks for supplies to rebuild the walls and gate of the city, and for his own house. This request might be the most dangerous of all because it was not just a financial decision, it was a political one. About thirteen years prior, Artaxerxes had given Ezra a lot of money to rebuild the temple (Ezra 7:11-26). Since then, the enemies of Israel had pressured him into changing his foreign policy about Israel to not help them. Nehemiah is asking the king to change his policies again! He is asking him to look like he is waffling! Under Persian law, even one "change of mind" was not allowed. Yet again, the mercy of God prevails, and the king gives him access to all he needs.

Basically, Nehemiah has asked for an almost indefinite leave of absence, a military escort, and the king's credit card. He has asked for all of this with the king getting nothing in return. What would *you* say if you were Artaxerxes?

The king's answer is amazing. The king granted Nehemiah everything he asked for! What mercy!

As we rebuild our lives and increase our service to the Lord, we will be going places we have never been, doing things we have never done, and needing things we have not needed before. We should not worry about the details. God has called us to action, and He knows what we need to fulfill our calling. We need to be very specific sometimes in prayer. When we are, and God answers, that assures us that it is God Who leads us and provides for us.

The spiritual application from this story teaches us several things. We are to pray before we act, and pray *while* we act. Once we have determined the will of God, we are to act courageously and overcome our fears. If we act in faith, God will move kings' hearts to grant us everything we need.

Face fear with faith!

Build your wall...

How often should we pray? Explain.

How specific should we be in our prayers?

The king granted Nehemiah some very large requests. This showed God's involvement. How big a request can we make to God?

9 • The Trip Home

"Then I came to the governors beyond the river, and gave them the king's letters. Now the king had sent captains of the army and horsemen with me. When Sanballat the Horonite, and Tobiah the servant, the Ammonite, heard of it, it grieved them exceedingly that there was come a man to seek the welfare of the children of Israel. So I came to Jerusalem, and was there three days." – Nehemiah 2:9-11

Nehemiah, having been blessed by the Lord to receive all he asked of the king, ventures home on what was probably a four-to-five-month-long journey (Ezra 7:8,9). He had letters in hand to show the area governors that he had permission to pass through their jurisdiction to return to Jerusalem. To back up those letters, Nehemiah also had a military escort to enforce the king's letters and keep them safe.

On the way, Nehemiah and his companions meet two of Israel's most vengeful enemies, Sanballat and Tobiah. These men were governors appointed or allowed by Artaxerxes to oversee their respective regions. Sanballat was the commander of a garrison of forces to the north of Judah in the area of Samaria. Tobiah had a similar position to the east of Jerusalem. He was close friends (or business partners) with Eliashib, a Jew in Jerusalem, whose grandson had married the daughter of Sanballat. Both Sanballat and Tobiah had leased storerooms in the Temple and made other deals with the ruling nobles in Jerusalem (Nehemiah 6:17; 13:4; 13:28). They did not view themselves as servants to Artaxerxes except when necessary. They were in charge and didn't like anyone messing with their set-up. The two had a very comfortable living as the neighborhood bullies of Judea.

And now a new sheriff is coming to town, and he wants to break up their unrighteous hold on Jerusalem and Israel. Nehemiah's very presence sets up the region for war.

It is interesting to note that Nehemiah does not record any initial meeting he had with these two wicked men. He has his eyes focused on his duty and will not let anything cause him fear or distract him from the goal. So, he travels home, and then rests up a few days before beginning his work.

In our spiritual journey, we are going to need to repent and rebuild portions of our lives. This will lead us to return to the word of God and church. It requires us to do this and other things that some people won't like. There are people who hate God, seemingly for no apparent reason, and they will do anything to stop the kingdom. There are others, who may be close to us or even related to us that also do not like the "new" way we are conducting our lives. When we have prepared our hearts in prayer and are trusting the Lord is with us, we need to ignore these distractions and move toward our goal.

And take a little rest before the true work starts.

Build your wall...

- When we start to follow the Lord, what does Satan think about that? What does he do?

- How concerned should we be about the popularity of Christianity or our personal discipleship?

- What are some good sources of encouragement as we seek to rebuild parts of our lives?

10 • Surveying the Damage

"And I arose in the night, I and some few men with me; neither told I any man what my God had put in my heart to do at Jerusalem: neither was there any beast with me, save the beast that I rode upon. And I went out by night by the gate of the valley, even before the dragon well, and to the dung port, and viewed the walls of Jerusalem, which were broken down, and the gates thereof were consumed with fire. Then I went on to the gate of the fountain, and to the king's pool: but there was no place for the beast that was under me to pass. Then went I up in the night by the brook, and viewed the wall, and turned back, and entered by the gate of the valley, and so returned. And the rulers knew not whither I went, or what I did; neither had I as yet told it to the Jews, nor to the priests, nor to the nobles, nor to the rulers, nor to the rest that did the work." – Nehemiah 2:12-16

Some might think that Nehemiah's next step is a bit unusual. I know I did, at first. With such a daunting task ahead of him, one would think he would immediately ask for help, at least to ease the burden of planning and preparation. But Nehemiah tells no one the plan. But that's the key, it was not *his* plan. The plan was God's, and HE put it on Nehemiah's heart. Nehemiah knows that he has the responsibility of overseeing the entire work. He knows that he needs to be intimately familiar with every detail of what needs to be done.

What he found was a city in ruins. Portions of the walls were destroyed to the extent that the donkey he rode upon could not even pass through.

Nehemiah probably anticipated opposition to his plan both from the outside, with Sanballat and Tobiah, and from the inside with the nobles that liked their current way of life, fellowshipping the heathen nations around them. Knowing that he would face such great opposition, he may have needed this time alone to inspect the damage: not only so he could see what needed to be done, but be fully persuaded that it *must* be done so nothing could change his mind. He needed to become like the old cartoon character, Popeye, when he had finally had enough, "That's all I can stand. I can't stands no more!"

When the Lord places a burden on our hearts to do something: it is *our* responsibility, not another's. If you see someone in need and you have the means to help, you don't need a charitable organization or anything else. Just help them.

Acting on faith does not require a committee. It requires a faithful disciple willing to take the first step. We may find that we need help understanding *how* to help someone, but the actual responsibility of the work is our own. We should understand what God has called us to do and be 100% engaged in the work.

Build your wall...

✕ What are some things that God calls individuals to do in the world?

✕ What are some things that God calls families, churches, etc. to do?

✕ Is it someone else's fault that you sin? Is it someone else's responsibility to repent and rebuild your life?

✕ Even after we repent, are there still things that require work to repair our lives?

11 • Damage Report

"Then said I unto them, Ye see the distress that we are in, how Jerusalem lieth waste, and the gates thereof are burned with fire: come, and let us build up the wall of Jerusalem, that we be no more a reproach. Then I told them of the hand of my God which was good upon me; as also the king's words that he had spoken unto me. And they said, Let us rise up and build. So they strengthened their hands for this good work. But when Sanballat the Horonite, and Tobiah the servant, the Ammonite, and Geshem the Arabian, heard it, they laughed us to scorn, and despised us, and said, What is this thing that ye do? will ye rebel against the king? Then answered I them, and said unto them, The God of heaven, he will prosper us; therefore we his servants will arise and build: but ye have no portion, nor right, nor memorial, in Jerusalem." – Nehemiah 2:17-20

Everybody knew there was a problem, but, to that date, no one had the courage or wisdom to fix it.

Nehemiah had been an intercessor as he mourned and prayed for the sins of his people and the condition of their city. He had been an amazing lobbyist, convincing Artaxerxes to change his political position on Israel and help them rebuild. Nehemiah, then, became a scout leader of military troops, supplies, and people as he led them back to Judea. He went out at night, changing hats again, and became a master architect with the plans to rebuild.

Now, Nehemiah must do what might be the most difficult task of all: motivate people to action and work!

But, as the Lord blessed every other step Nehemiah took, He blesses him once again. The fire of one man moved a nation. He showed his passion. He showed what God had told him to do. He showed them the evidence of the providence of God in what the king said and did for him. He basically cried out, "What are we waiting for?!?" And the people responded,

Let us rise up and build!

Even when Geshem, a third enemy, showed up from the south, completing the circle of enemies around them, Nehemiah does not waver. He turns to Sanballat and Tobiah and tells them to get their stuff out of the Temple and get themselves out of Jerusalem. Rather than cowering at the sight of another enemy, Nehemiah kicks the others out of town!

We all need spiritual leaders in our lives. Of course, we should seek the will of God in the study of His word, but we need good pastors to guide us and give us instruction. The world will always mock righteous reform. Mock and ridicule are Satan's first volley of fiery darts. Did we think the devil was going to just give up and go home simply because we showed up?

What happens if we are not in the *shield of faith* of a good Bible church? The church must be in strong unity and fellowship to fight off the devil and build the foundation and walls of the Christian life.

And remember, the first step to recovery is to **kick out the invaders!**

Build your wall...

⚒ How do you respond when someone points out to you something that needs to improve in your life?

⚒ What help(s) do we have when trying to rebuild?

⚒ How do we handle verbal mocking and ridicule?

12 • Who Are All These People?

Please Read Nehemiah Chapter 3.

When I began preparing my commentary on this chapter, I looked back at my notes and saw a theme. But it was an unusual one. It contained phrases such as "not much is known about these people," "little known," and a host of just empty spaces with question marks. I got a little concerned. I mean, why would God give us a list of workers whom we knew little or nothing about? There are even groups in the list that have no name or lineage at all! I like to know who people are, and this bothered me, *at first*.

Then, I realized what the Holy Spirit is pointing out, "IT'S NOT ABOUT YOU!" The point of the rebuilding of the wall in Jerusalem was for the glory of God, not the people. The point of our existence is not for our glory, it is for God's glory and the beauty of Christ's Bride, the church.

In this chapter, we will find a few precious gems of information about individuals or families. From these we can learn some great spiritual and practical lessons. But we must never miss the big picture shown in this chapter. The people banded together, each working on their portion of the wall according to their abilities. Each did their part, seemingly separate from the others. But Nehemiah's account shows how it all came together, starting and ending in the same place.

And so it is in our personal and church lives. We each have a personal responsibility to serve the Lord every day and through our home church. But we must never forget, we are one in Christ. Our duties are done for the glory of God and the benefit of the body of Christ.

> *"I therefore, the prisoner of the Lord, beseech you that ye walk worthy of the vocation wherewith ye are called, With all lowliness and meekness, with longsuffering, forbearing one another in love; Endeavouring to keep the unity of the Spirit in the bond of peace."*
>
> *– Ephesians 4:1-3*

We all are anonymous, yet vital, children of God!

Build your wall...

✗ How important is it for others to notice our discipleship?

✗ Compare social media posts about good works to the Pharisees sounding a trumpet so everyone looks at them.

✗ How small does a role in the church or family have to be in order to not be vital?

13 • Hard Work Never Hurt Anybody

"Then Eliashib the high priest rose up with his brethren the priests, and they builded the sheep gate; they sanctified it, and set up the doors of it; even unto the tower of Meah they sanctified it, unto the tower of Hananeel." – Nehemiah 3:1

I remember a time when I was young, and we went and visited an old country church. We went into the sanctuary and found the pastor, an elderly gentleman, vacuuming the carpet. I told him I was surprised to see him doing this in there. He responded, "With me, you don't just get preaching. You get vacuuming, dish washing, mowing. You get it all." I have never forgotten the impression that had on me. I hope I never forget that lesson as I try to pastor the congregation the Lord has placed in my care.

In this verse we see something very striking. The priests did not sit out. They took responsibility for their portion of the wall and worked.

It is fitting that the spiritual leaders would also lead by *example* in the physical work.

It is fitting also that the priests would work on the sheep gate. This is the area where sacrifices were let into the city and taken to be washed and sacrificed in the Temple. This is why sanctification of the area was necessary. Nehemiah shows that all rebuilding projects in our lives must begin at the cross of Christ!

It is fitting to see the religious leaders lead by example. In this modern era of corporate mentality in the church, I think we can easily lose focus on our purpose and duty to God and his people in our church.

Fellow pastors, let us not be guilty of teaching our flock to do what we say and not what we do. Let us lead by example.

> *"And next unto him builded the men of Jericho. And next to them builded Zaccur the son of Imri. But the fish gate did the sons of Hassenaah build, who also laid the beams thereof, and set up the doors thereof, the locks thereof, and the bars thereof. And next unto them repaired Meremoth the son of Urijah, the son of Koz. And next unto them repaired Meshullam the son of Berechiah, the son of Meshezabeel. And next unto them repaired Zadok the son of Baana. And next unto them the Tekoites repaired; but their nobles put not their necks to the work of their Lord." – Nehemiah 3:2-5*

The next few verses give us little detail beyond a few names and the location of their portion of the reconstruction. Meremoth is mentioned in Ezra 8:33. He made the vessels of gold for the temple. Other than that, we don't have a lot of information. These remind us that our service, at times, is basically anonymous. Although anonymous, each of us is *vital* in the Lord's service.

The remarkable point in this passage, however, is not who was working but who was *not* working. Among the Tekoites, there were some very rich people. These *nobles* felt that hard labor in stone and wood was beneath them. Moreover, they would not even give money to hire workers or buy supplies. They were completely against the rebuilding effort! What a disgrace.

We will see the Tekoites again in a later verse. Clearly, the regular folks among them didn't follow the nobles' arrogant example. They finish their portion of the wall and then go help others to finish. Now, that is true nobility!

When you think about it, people who are more affluent actually have *more* and easier opportunities to help in the Lord's work. They can give more, but the typical pattern is that many give less percentage-wise than the more humble members of the congregation. They can also spend more time physically doing things for the church. The boss can have a lot more discretion for days to be off from work than the average worker. Now, before anyone accuses me of just bashing rich people, consider this. This sense of *nobility* is not limited to people who are actually rich. Anytime people feel that a particular job is below them, they have forgotten their Savior and become like these Tekoite nobles.

We need to have the mind of Christ:

> *"Let this mind be in you, which was also in Christ Jesus: Who, being in the form of God, thought it not robbery to be equal with God: But made himself of no reputation, and took upon him the form of a servant, and was made in the likeness of men: And being found in fashion as a man, he humbled himself, and became obedient unto death, even the death of the cross." – Philippians 2:5-8*

Don't just *go* to church. *Be* the church.

Build you wall...

- Who all should be involved in family, church rebuilding?

- How often do you think about church when you are not in a worship service?

- What is more important, the amount of money we donate to a cause or the amount of time and effort?

14 • It's All in the Details

"Moreover the old gate repaired Jehoiada the son of Paseah, and Meshullam the son of Besodeiah; they laid the beams thereof, and set up the doors thereof, and the locks thereof, and the bars thereof. And next unto them repaired Melatiah the Gibeonite, and Jadon the Meronothite, the men of Gibeon, and of Mizpah, unto the throne of the governor on this side the river." – Nehemiah 3:6-7

Not much is known about the families and tribes that worked on this next portion of the wall. They are blessed to be among the *AYV's* of this reconstruction.

These **A**nonymous **Y**et **V**ital children of God did the work for the glory of God and the edification of Israel. And they did it to the smallest detail; from the beams, to the doors, to the locks, and to the bars. They didn't start the work and then leave off when they got bored or it got difficult. They finished their jobs, and they finished them to the tiniest detail.

Consider what detail God used in the flowers of the field. Jesus taught us that our Heavenly Father cares that much about the details of our lives as well. Should we not, then, dedicate as much attention to detail in our labors for the Lord in our family and church?

He gave His only begotten Son for us. We owe Him our lives. We owe Him more than just a couple of hours on Sunday morning. We owe Him every word, deed, step, dollar, and breath. And not only that, we owe Him a joyful and thankful countenance as we serve in His kingdom.

We should strive to be faithful in all the little details of our discipleship. For when we do, we are faithful in much. If we have had a problem with regular attendance at church or reading our Bible, we should dedicate ourselves to doing more. We might think this a small thing, but a faithful disciple does small things every day. And those *small* things change lives and glorify God!

Build your wall...

X. How much of our lives do we owe to God?

X. What does a life totally devoted to God look like?

X. Can children have a significant role in church or family improvement? Explain.

X. What happens when you only partially renovate a building? How does this apply to our lives?

15 • We're All in the Same Boat

"Moreover the old gate repaired Jehoiada the son of Paseah, and Meshullam the son of Besodeiah; they laid the beams thereof, and set up the doors thereof, and the locks thereof, and the bars thereof. And next unto them repaired Melatiah the Gibeonite, and Jadon the Meronothite, the men of Gibeon, and of Mizpah, unto the throne of the governor on this side the river. Next unto him repaired Uzziel the son of Harhaiah, of the goldsmiths. Next unto him also repaired Hananiah the son of one of the apothecaries, and they fortified Jerusalem unto the broad wall. – Nehemiah 3:6-8

Verses 6 and 7 of Nehemiah, Chapter 3 offer few details, so we will just let them stand as they are. However, verse 8 gives us more to learn if we know a little history.

During the time the nation was divided into Israel and Judah, this portion of the wall was broken down by Joash, king of Israel. Men, who were supposed to be united in the service to the Lord, had become more self-serving than God-honoring. This resulted in wars from within, which can be more dangerous than attacks from the enemies of the world. This portion of the wall was rebuilt by

King Uzziah of Judah. At the time of Nehemiah, this wall was still intact so they fortified the city *unto* it.

Sometimes we have to rebuild, not from external attack but from the result of infighting. Our enemy is not within the church. We should war against the rulers of darkness not fellow children of God. We need to humble ourselves and seek unity.

Be careful about how much you shoot holes in someone else's boat. We are all in the same boat!

> *"And next unto them repaired Rephaiah the son of Hur, the ruler of the half part of Jerusalem. And next unto them repaired Jedaiah the son of Harumaph, even over against his house. And next unto him repaired Hattush the son of Hashabniah. Malchijah the son of Harim, and Hashub the son of Pahathmoab, repaired the other piece, and the tower of the furnaces. And next unto him repaired Shallum the son of Halohesh, the ruler of the half part of Jerusalem, he and his daughters."*
> *– Nehemiah 3:9-12*

These four verses teach us two very important lessons about our active involvement in church.

First of all, we see that this portion of Jerusalem was actually ruled by two different tribes. For the safety of each, the tribes had to come together in unity to rebuild this area of the wall. Everyone in church has different backgrounds and abilities. The Lord blesses each of His children in different ways intending them to work together for His glory and the edification of the body of Christ which is the church.

> *"From whom the whole body fitly joined together and compacted by that which every joint supplieth, according to the effectual working in the measure of every part, maketh increase of the body unto the edifying of itself in love."* *– Ephesians 4:16*

What gives the body its true strength is not each individual part. It is the joints coordinating all the parts that produce unified power. And so it is with the church. No individual is more important than another. It is the interpersonal relationships bringing gifts together that make a strong church.

Secondly, we can see that many of the families working on the wall had homes that were actually part of the wall or very close to it. As they worked to fortify the city, they were also protecting their own homes. The key to having a strong home and family is exactly the same. When we focus our family into church life, we build up our church and strengthen our families at the same time.

> *"And thou shalt teach them diligently unto thy children, and shalt talk of them when thou sittest in thine house, and when thou walkest by the way, and when thou liest down, and when thou risest up."*
>
> *– Deuteronomy 6:7*

History has shown throughout all generations that the vitality of the church depends on the strength of family devotion. Also, time has proven that steadfast and loving families are best nurtured by a deep devotion to the Lord in public worship. The church and family have a wondrous symbiotic relationship where they feed and empower one another, just as God designed it!

Build your wall...

- Who is the most important member of your family or church?

- According to the Ephesian quote above, what is more important for family or church growth, individual effort or cooperative relationships?

- Describe something in your life that you had to rebuild because you broke it down yourself.

16 • Anonymous Yet Vital

"And next unto him repaired Shallum the son of Halohesh, the ruler of the half part of Jerusalem, he and his daughters. The valley gate repaired Hanun, and the inhabitants of Zanoah; they built it, and set up the doors thereof, the locks thereof, and the bars thereof, and a thousand cubits on the wall unto the dung gate."
– Nehemiah 3:12-13

In rebuilding the walls of Jerusalem, as in all projects, there are very visible portions of the work and other areas that are more behind the scenes. These two verses, while seeming to just add to the list of workers, actually present us with two groups of ***Anonymous Yet Vital*** workers in this project.

Halohesh apparently had no sons, or his sons chose to not take part in the rebuilding effort. Either way, we find a rare occurrence in scripture when the *daughters* of someone are mentioned. Genealogies and other important events typically only list the sons of those involved. So when we have daughters mentioned, we should take note.

According to customs of the time, we should not assume that these daughters actually took part in the physical labor of the rebuild. Rather, they were most likely wealthy, and they hired workers to do the work in their family name. Why is this important? As you might recall, the nobles of the Tekoites refused to work or even support the rebuilding effort. This is mentioned to their shame. Here, these faithful, though unnamed, daughters are mentioned to show that, even though they could not physically partake in the work effort, they supported the work by any means they could. Not everyone can do the same thing, but everyone *can* do something!

These daughters, along with the next group mentioned, might easily be overlooked because they don't repair a prominent gate or structure. As a matter of fact, their portions lead up to the dung gate. And the function of that gate is exactly what it sounds like. That's not exactly the kind of picture you put on the postcard for your city, but look at the importance of their portion of the work. This wall is probably over 1,500 feet long, and it is on a portion of the city that seems unimportant. That is a huge area that could very well be the best place for any enemy to make a breach in the wall and infiltrate the city! Although their work didn't look that important, it was crucial to the defense of the city.

Discipleship in our churches works exactly the same way. Each member has been blessed by God with certain gifts or abilities. Some of these gifts make the person more visible and prominent in the congregation. But this does not mean that he or she is *more* important. Visibility is just the nature of their particular job. All work in the church is vital to the health and safety of the church.

If we *seek* a more visible position, perhaps we should examine *why* we seek that position. Is it for the notoriety or the credit that we would receive? If so, we should reexamine our motivation and seek the good of the church rather than the promotion of our own reputation.

Remember what Jesus taught when the disciples disputed about who would be greatest in the kingdom:

> *"Whosoever therefore shall humble himself as this little child, the same is greatest in the kingdom of heaven." – Matthew 18:4*

Build your wall...

⚒ Do you want to be helpful or visible in your service to God?

⚒ Do the various roles of men and women described by God make one group more important than the other?

⚒ Are ability gifts given to the children of God for recognition or for service?

⚒ If family or church members are fighting, who is winning?

17 • All Jobs Are Important in the House of God

"But the dung gate repaired Malchiah the son of Rechab, the ruler of part of Bethhaccerem; he built it, and set up the doors thereof, the locks thereof, and the bars thereof." – Nehemiah 3:14

The area of the dung gate was as nasty as it sounds. It was the portal used for all sorts of refuse and trash to be dumped outside the city. It was not exactly the most coveted portion of the wall to rebuild.

Moreover, if these people were the Rechabites mentioned in Jeremiah, Chapter 35, they weren't even allowed to build themselves permanent personal houses. They were sentenced to live in tents on the outside of the city. But they were faithful. Even though they were not going to be able to enjoy the comfort and security of the city, they knew they had a part in its rebuilding. They were more concerned about the wellbeing of the city than they were of themselves.

What an amazing example for us! Not only did these folks have the nastiest place to repair, they were not even going to benefit much from the reconstruction! The glory of God and the edification of His church should be the focus of our efforts. We should not work for what we will get out of it, but for the benefit of others. Also, no job is beneath us! We should be like the prodigal son:

*"I will arise and go to my father, and will say unto him, Father, I have
sinned against heaven, and before thee, And am no more worthy to be
called thy son: make me as one of thy hired servants."*
– Luke 15:18-19

We have no righteousness to stand on or glory to claim as our own. It is by God's
grace that we have any part in the kingdom. Our humility gives God all the glory.
Let us rejoice in God's glory, not our own.

The next several verses in Nehemiah, Chapter 3 describe the repair work done
to some of the more prominent structures in Jerusalem. Several of these areas can
be identified even as late as the times of the New Testament.

*"But the gate of the fountain repaired Shallun the son of Colhozeh, the
ruler of part of Mizpah; he built it, and covered it, and set up the doors
thereof, the locks thereof, and the bars thereof, and the wall of the pool
of Siloah by the king's garden, and unto the stairs that go down from
the city of David." – Nehemiah 3:15*

This verse describes the repair of the fountain gate that was completed to the last
detail including something that was not recorded at any of the previous gates.
This one had a covering or roof. This area used to be outside the city wall, but it
appears Manasseh enclosed the area for the king's garden (1 Chr. 33:14).

*"After him repaired Nehemiah the son of Azbuk, the ruler of the half
part of Bethzur, unto the place over against the sepulchres of David,
and to the pool that was made, and unto the house of the mighty." –
Nehemiah 3:16*

Verse 16 tells about another man named Nehemiah who repaired around the
pool made by Hezekiah (2 Kings 20:20). This area also included the burial area
where King David's body was laid to rest. This area was still intact during the
New Testament times (Acts 2:29). This is a *very* important structure. Peter
points to David's sepulcher during his sermon in Acts, Chapter 2 proving that
David spoke prophetically about the resurrection of the Messiah from the dead.

*"After him repaired the Levites, Rehum the son of Bani. Next unto
him repaired Hashabiah, the ruler of the half part of Keilah, in his
part. After him repaired their brethren, Bavai the son of Henadad, the
ruler of the half part of Keilah. And next to him repaired Ezer the son
of Jeshua, the ruler of Mizpah, another piece over against the going up
to the armoury at the turning of the wall." – Nehemiah 3:17-19*

Verses 17 through 19 record the work of the Levites in their own neighborhood and the wall that surrounded it. The armory is alluded to in Song of Solomon, Chapter 4.

It is interesting to notice that there are several areas in Jerusalem that concern the Levites and/or the Temple. This is significant for us to understand. The focus of the Jewish life was the Temple. Jesus Christ made the final perfect offering of Himself for our sins. Therefore, the focus is removed from the Temple and should be on Him and His church to the same degree. We should be as devoted to the Lord through our church as the Jews were to the Temple in Jerusalem.

The church is the bride of Christ. When we meet together, it is the most important place on earth!

Build your wall...

- How concerned should we be about "what we will get out of" our service to God?

- How does pride or lack of humility rob God of His glory?

- Compare/Contrast your personal devotion to your local church with the devotion the Levites had toward the Temple.

- Name services that you could do for your church, family, or community.

18 • Good "Earnest" Work

"After him Baruch the son of Zabbai earnestly repaired the other piece, from the turning of the wall unto the door of the house of Eliashib the high priest. After him repaired Meremoth the son of Urijah the son of Koz another piece, from the door of the house of Eliashib even to the end of the house of Eliashib. And after him repaired the priests, the men of the plain. After him repaired Benjamin and Hashub over against their house. After him repaired Azariah the son of Maaseiah the son of Ananiah by his house. After him repaired Binnui the son of Henadad another piece, from the house of Azariah unto the turning of the wall, even unto the corner. Palal the son of Uzai, over against the turning of the wall, and the tower which lieth out from the king's high house, that was by the court of the prison. After him Pedaiah the son of Parosh. Moreover the Nethinims dwelt in Ophel, unto the place over against the water gate toward the east, and the tower that lieth out. After them the Tekoites repaired another piece, over against the great tower that lieth out, even unto the wall of Ophel. From above the horse gate repaired the priests, every one over against his house. After them repaired Zadok the son of Immer over against his house. After him repaired also Shemaiah the son of Shechaniah, the keeper of the east gate. After him repaired Hananiah the son of Shelemiah, and

*Hanun the sixth son of Zalaph, another piece. After him repaired
Meshullam the son of Berechiah over against his chamber."*
– Nehemiah 3:20-30

We will look at a much larger portion of Scripture in today's study because there is an overarching theme that unites several of these workers. The level of devotion shown by these men is an excellent example for us to follow in our *active* service to the Lord.

In verse 20, a man named Baruch is said to *earnestly* repair his portion of the wall. The Hebrew word for *earnestly* bears multiple meanings from anger to heated behavior. I think the latter most likely applies here. If we were to see this man working today, we would say, "He is working like a mad man on that wall!" Oh, if we could only be accused of such behavior in our devotion to God and His church!

Also notice in this verse that it was the portion of the wall where Eliashib's house was, but he was not working on that part. The high priest had a more important job in the Temple so he was working on that part. Our ministers today need to have that kind of liberty to work their *primary* job, the gospel ministry.

In verse 21, we come across a name we have heard before. Meremoth apparently was such a hard worker that he finished his part (Neh. 3:4) and came here to help finish. Verse 27 records the same thing about the Tekoites. Remember, their nobles would not work nor would they spend their riches for materials or workers for their portion of the responsibility. These Tekoites, however, not only overcame the lazy arrogance of their nobles, they finished early and were able to help out on another part! What a great testimony and example these folks are. Their focus was not on themselves. It was not even just on their part of the job. They wanted everyone to succeed for the glory of Jerusalem!

The next several verses contain more **Anonymous Yet Vital** workers. Each family was working diligently on their portion of the wall. The Nethenims were servants of the Temple. They had the responsibility of bringing water to the Temple. Therefore, they worked on that gate. Some of those listed here don't even include a family name!

Verse 30 speaks about a man that has this same *earnest* work ethic as the Tekoites and Meremoth. Zalaph had six sons (possibly more) but only Hanun showed up to work. He ignored the bad example of his five older brothers and led his family in the good work of rebuilding the wall!

We may be blessed with good examples of service in our earthly families. But even if we are not, we have men like Baruch, Hanun, Meremoth, and the Tekoites to show us that we can do great things in the kingdom of God! Regardless of the actual examples we have in our earthly families or among the church brethren, we have Biblical examples to follow and a command to be about our Father's business, *earnestly*!

Build your wall...

- Describe what usually happens when we procrastinate in our service to the Lord.

- If others are not willing to work, should that change our work ethic? Explain.

- Name some Biblical examples of hard workers. Name some people you know that are hard workers.

19 • Full Circle

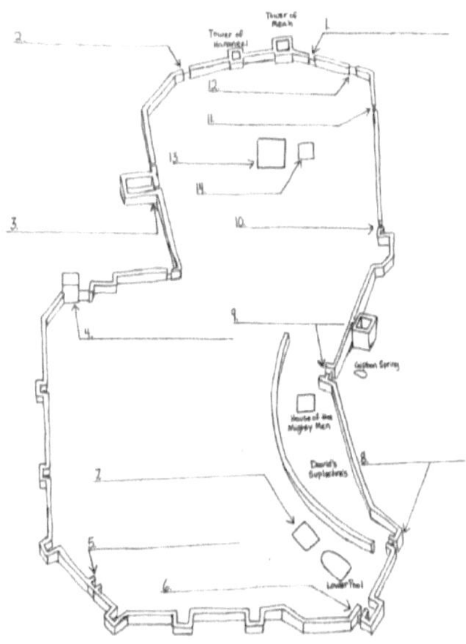

> "After him repaired Malchiah the goldsmith's son unto the place of the Nethinims, and of the merchants, over against the gate Miphkad, and to the going up of the corner. And between the going up of the corner unto the sheep gate repaired the goldsmiths and the merchants."
> — Nehemiah 3:31-32

In these final two verses, we find ourselves back around to the sheep gate once again. These areas seem to be some of the most ornate portions of the wall seeing that the goldsmiths and merchants are working here. This area is most likely where the Sanhedrin court would have met during Paul's time.

The most significant thing that we should learn from these verses is that Nehemiah has been listing the duties of each group around the perimeter of the city. Each section was assigned to a group, and they all worked at the same time. It was important to have the entire wall complete with each portion being finished roughly at the same time. This made the city more secure. Had they only worked on sections one at a time, enemies could have slowed their work by attacking them through one of the other breaches in the wall.

When we apply this to our lives spiritually, we see that we need to work on the whole man, not just one or two aspects at a time. Paul told us in Romans, Chapter 12 to present our *bodies* as a living sacrifice, not just an arm or a foot. When Jesus called His disciples, we see that they immediately stopped what they were doing and devoted their entire life to Him.

Our devotion to God must have this *all in* attitude. When we work with other church members, each person needs to have that same devotion.

Build your wall...

- What does an *all in* attitude toward the Lord look like?

- Describe what would have happened if Israel had only rebuilt a portion of the wall around Jerusalem. How does this relate to repentance and discipleship?

- How dangerous is this statement – "I'm doing enough"?

20 • Nothing but Bullies and Troubles

"But it came to pass, that when Sanballat heard that we builded the wall, he was wroth, and took great indignation, and mocked the Jews. And he spake before his brethren and the army of Samaria, and said, What do these feeble Jews? will they fortify themselves? will they sacrifice? will they make an end in a day? will they revive the stones out of the heaps of the rubbish which are burned? Now Tobiah the Ammonite was by him, and he said, Even that which they build, if a fox go up, he shall even break down their stone wall. Hear, O our God; for we are despised: and turn their reproach upon their own head, and give them for a prey in the land of captivity. And cover not their iniquity, and let not their sin be blotted out from before thee: for they have provoked thee to anger before the builders. So built we the wall; and all the wall was joined together unto the half thereof: for the people had a mind to work." – Nehemiah 4:1-6

As soon as they began to work, the enemies of God started mocking the Israelites. Remember, if someone hates God, they hate His people too!

The bullies, who had been in charge of the area for many years, did not like the new kids coming in to rebuild. The tactic they used to try to discourage the Israelites is very similar to what bullies still do. They say hurtful things and make fun of others. In the eyes of a bully, he sees himself as better when he can bring everyone else down. Typically, there is no substance to anything they say, but this technique is very effective in making someone worry about how others view them.

Sanballat and the others call the Israelites names and ridicule the rebuilding effort. They mock that the job to rebuild is an impossible one, and the building skills of the Israelites is so poor that even the lightest of animals could knock it down.

The effectiveness of these gang-mentality techniques lies completely within the one being mocked. Everything that is happening is just words, no truth or threat. The best thing to do is ignore it. But Nehemiah and his fellow Israelites do one better. They pray.

They prayed that Sanballat and the others would be taken captive just like they were. They don't point out personal pride as the reason. They see that this mocking is actually against God and not just them. They ask God to go ahead and act out in His anger toward them!

Then notice what happens next. They don't sit and whine because they are being mocked. They don't stop working and wait for the Lord to destroy their enemies. They ignore the reproach, leave it in the hands of God, and get back to work.

There are going to be detractors who will seek to interrupt our walk with God. We don't need to waste a lot of time with them. We should just ignore their words, leave their situation in the hands of a righteous and all-powerful God, and then get back to serving the Lord. When we "have a mind" to work in the Lord's service, nothing can stand in our way!

"But it came to pass, that when Sanballat, and Tobiah, and the Arabians, and the Ammonites, and the Ashdodites, heard that the walls of Jerusalem were made up, and that the breaches began to be stopped, then they were very wroth, And conspired all of them together to come and to fight against Jerusalem, and to hinder it. Nevertheless we made our prayer unto our God, and set a watch against them day and night, because of them. And Judah said, The strength of the bearers of burdens is decayed, and there is much rubbish; so that we are not able to build the wall. And our adversaries said, They shall not

know, neither see, till we come in the midst among them, and slay them, and cause the work to cease. And it came to pass, that when the Jews which dwelt by them came, they said unto us ten times, From all places whence ye shall return unto us they will be upon you."
— Nehemiah 4:7-12

When they realized that their bully technique of mocking the Israelites was not working, Sanballat and the others gather more friends into their gang and make plans to attack Jerusalem and stop the work. On top of that, the trash from the reconstruction is piling up because those that bear that burden have grown weary. And on top of that, rumors from fellow Jews are telling them that Sanballat and his thugs are going to smother them with an attack before they even know they are there!

It looks absolutely hopeless! Or does it? The Israelites seem to ignore these threats as well. They pray, they set a guard, and like the Energizer Bunny, they just keep going and going!

When we get discouraged in our Christian walk, it can sometimes feel like there is more trouble around every turn. It seems like every time we do something right, there is another obstacle trying to block our path. We are not hallucinating when we see this happening. The devil really hates it when we follow God. When we do good, the devil does everything he can to stop us! We can take a lesson from the courage of Nehemiah and these Israelites. They kept praying, and they kept marching on. So can we!

Build your wall...

⚒ Does the devil give up when we decide to follow the Lord? Explain.

⚒ What is the best thing to do with distractions to your discipleship?

⚒ Describe how peer pressure could be good or bad.

21 • Build and Defend

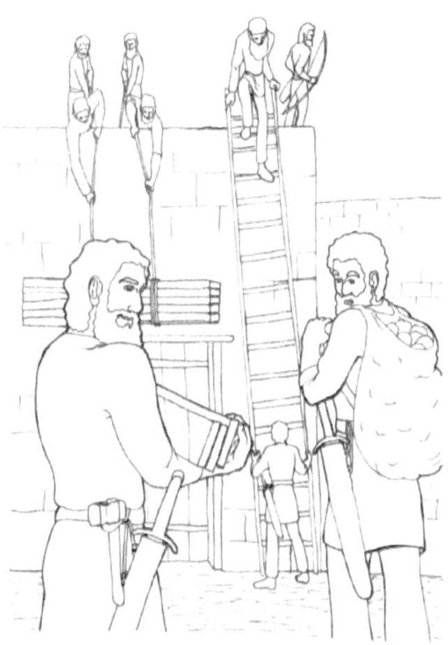

"Therefore set I in the lower places behind the wall, and on the higher places, I even set the people after their families with their swords, their spears, and their bows. And I looked, and rose up, and said unto the nobles, and to the rulers, and to the rest of the people, Be not ye afraid of them: remember the Lord, which is great and terrible, and fight for your brethren, your sons, and your daughters, your wives, and your houses. And it came to pass, when our enemies heard that it was known unto us, and God had brought their counsel to nought, that we returned all of us to the wall, every one unto his work. And it came to pass from that time forth, that the half of my servants wrought in the work, and the other half of them held both the spears, the shields, and the bows, and the habergeons; and the rulers were behind all the house of Judah. They which builded on the wall, and they that bare burdens, with those that laded, every one with one of his hands wrought in the work, and with the other hand held a weapon. For the builders, every one had his sword girded by his side, and so builded. And he that sounded the trumpet was by me." – Nehemiah 4:13-18

When it seemed like everything that could come against them had come against them, the Israelites remained strong. We need to remember that Nehemiah was working and suffering right alongside his fellow countrymen. Yet he remained their steadfast leader and exhorted them to continue on. He reminded them that God is terrible to His enemies and that they should keep building for the safety of their own families.

Their courage was blessed by the Lord. Sanballat learned that Israel had found out his plan to attack, so he called it off. Nehemiah then adjusted the rebuilding plans to include defense measures as well. Everyone had their building assignments and a sword.

They had to be tired, but they knew how important the work was.

We must remember to always be aware of possible attacks from Satan. Jesus warned us that the devil goes about like a roaring lion seeking whom he may devour (1st Peter 5:8). As we build up our lives and our families' lives in the Lord, Satan gets all the more enraged. Thankfully, the Lord has provided us with a sword. The sword of the Spirit, which is the word of God, will help us fight our battles and maintain our walk in Christ. The Lord gave us the sword, all we need to do is pick it up and read it!

> *"And I said unto the nobles, and to the rulers, and to the rest of the people, The work is great and large, and we are separated upon the wall, one far from another. In what place therefore ye hear the sound of the trumpet, resort ye thither unto us: our God shall fight for us. So we laboured in the work: and half of them held the spears from the rising of the morning till the stars appeared. Likewise at the same time said I unto the people, Let every one with his servant lodge within Jerusalem, that in the night they may be a guard to us, and labour on the day. So neither I, nor my brethren, nor my servants, nor the men of the guard which followed me, none of us put off our clothes, saving that every one put them off for washing." – Nehemiah 4:19-23*

Nehemiah, like all good leaders, does not ignore the severity of their situation. He tells it like it is. "The work is hard and we are stretched too thin to complete the work and defend ourselves." He devises an early warning system where trumpeters would sound the alarm when an attack was coming. Defenders from other parts of the city would then come and lend help to thwart off any attack. This added threat of attack also made it necessary to sleep in their work clothes, with their weapons on the job site. They also brought in those who lived outside the city to protect them at night. They were willing to do whatever was necessary to finish the work.

Sometimes our service to the Lord is very demanding. But when the danger is so threatening, we must be willing to make personal sacrifices of comfort to ensure that our families are safe from the dangers of the world. And that is the key to remember, the danger *is that* threatening, It cannot be ignored. The enemy *will* try to discourage through mocking and peer pressure. He *will* try to sneak in through the media we watch and read. He *will* threaten us, and possibly even wage a full attack on us.

We must be ready!

Vigilant prayer, Bible study, and active church life are our keys to a strong defense.

Build your wall...

- Is the effort to rebuild our life, family, or church a one-time event? Explain

- Describe ways Satan attacks while we are trying to do right.

22 • Troubles Within

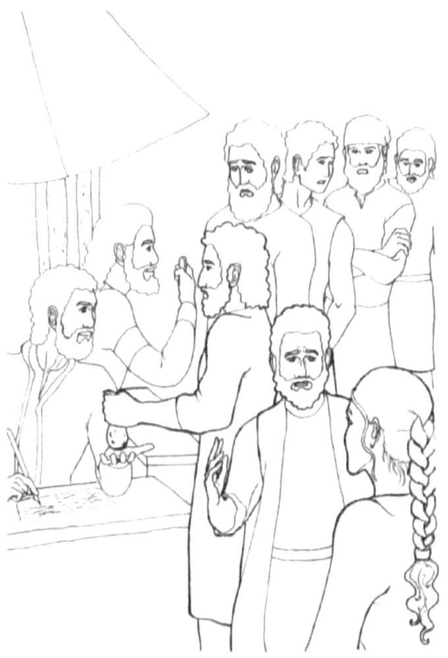

"And there was a great cry of the people and of their wives against their brethren the Jews. For there were that said, We, our sons, and our daughters, are many: therefore we take up corn for them, that we may eat, and live. Some also there were that said, We have mortgaged our lands, vineyards, and houses, that we might buy corn, because of the dearth. There were also that said, We have borrowed money for the king's tribute, and that upon our lands and vineyards. Yet now our flesh is as the flesh of our brethren, our children as their children: and, lo, we bring into bondage our sons and our daughters to be servants, and some of our daughters are brought unto bondage already: neither is it in our power to redeem them; for other men have our lands and vineyards." – Nehemiah 5:1-5

The work on the wall was continuing well, despite their enemies' best efforts to discourage them. However, when trouble brews up from within, it can be a far more dangerous enemy!

There was a drought or some other natural problem that caused crops to fail that year. All sorts of grain were being sold at a hefty price. The nobles of the Jews were able to buy up grain and were selling it at an even higher price to their fellow Jews that were poor. When the poor were unable to pay, the nobles would take property and land as collateral for a loan with a very high interest rate (usury). The problem got so bad that the poor had basically sold all their possessions and were selling their children as bondservants just to be able to buy food.

Even without the laws given to the Jews by God forbidding such practices, anyone can see that this is a cruel and horrible way to treat anyone, much less your own countrymen.

The poor came to Nehemiah and complained about what was going on. Needless to say, Nehemiah was *hopping mad* about this!

> *"And I was very angry when I heard their cry and these words."*
>
> *– Nehemiah 5:6*

As Christians, we are taught to take care of others as well as we care for ourselves, particularly within our own church congregation. Paul teaches it this way:

> *"Look not every man on his own things, but every man also on the things of others." – Philippians 2:4*

If we see someone in need, and we are able to help, we should help them. And do not charge interest on the loan! We should just *give* them what they need to help them get back on their feet. And not only this, if we see this punitive behavior happening, we should get angry, just like Nehemiah! Then, we should work to fix the problem immediately.

There are times when anger is a righteous thing. This is one of those times.

Build your wall...

✝ Should our personal needs come first or the needs of others?

✝ Describe how Jesus would answer the question above.

✝ Do we need to create new organizations or charities to help people in need?

23 • Naughty Nobles

"And I was very angry when I heard their cry and these words. Then I consulted with myself, and I rebuked the nobles, and the rulers, and said unto them, Ye exact usury, every one of his brother. And I set a great assembly against them. And I said unto them, We after our ability have redeemed our brethren the Jews, which were sold unto the heathen; and will ye even sell your brethren? or shall they be sold unto us? Then held they their peace, and found nothing to answer. Also I said, It is not good that ye do: ought ye not to walk in the fear of our God because of the reproach of the heathen our enemies? I likewise, and my brethren, and my servants, might exact of them money and corn: I pray you, let us leave off this usury. Restore, I pray you, to them, even this day, their lands, their vineyards, their oliveyards, and their houses, also the hundredth part of the money, and of the corn, the wine, and the oil, that ye exact of them. Then said they, We will restore them, and will require nothing of them; so will we do as thou sayest. Then I called the priests, and took an oath of them, that they should do according to this promise. Also I shook my lap, and said, So God shake out every man from his house, and from his labour, that performeth not this promise, even thus be he shaken out, and emptied. And all the congregation said, Amen, and praised the Lord. And the people did according to this promise." – Nehemiah 5:6-13

Nehemiah's solution to the fleecing of the poor by the nobles is simple. He confronts them directly, firmly, and with many witnesses against them. He tells them plainly that they are treating their fellow Jews just like the Babylonians and the Persians who held them in bondage. He sets forth a plan to repay the poor their losses and assure that they will have enough to live on through the drought. Then, he issues a warning of how God would treat those that would go back on their vow to do better. There was an overwhelmingly good response to this harsh rebuke. The people repented and united in praise to God!

Our modern view of sin has become both weak and judgmental at the same time. When we have sin discovered in ourselves, we *try* to justify it with terms other than "sin," and seek to give reasons and extenuating circumstances. The fact is, sin is sin, and we need to face up to our failures.

On the other hand, when we see sin in others, we are very quick to point it out and think ourselves better than those whose sins we have discovered.

What we need is a good dose of Nehemiah's plain-spoken rebuke and call for repentance. One of the main purposes of church is to encourage or *provoke* one another to good works and admonish one another when we step out of the way into sin.

> *"And let us consider one another to provoke unto love and to good works:" – Hebrews 10:24*

This work is not to declare who is a child of God or who is the most righteous. This work to discipline one another is for the purpose of bringing God more glory through our Christian walk. We need to humble ourselves. We each need to prefer our brother over ourselves. And we need to seek the glory of the kingdom rather than our own comfort and pleasure. What we really need every once in a while is a good kick in the pants and then make a *U-turn* in our lives.

Contrary to what the world may say, the Bible teaches us that when we actively help one another in Biblical discipline, it leads to *more* unity in the church, the church has true growth, and the Lord receives more glory!

Build your wall...

- Are there sins that other people do that you would never consider doing? Is it possible that you commit a sin that others would never think of?

- How do we help someone who is in sin without being judgmental?

24 • A Pattern for All Leaders

"Moreover from the time that I was appointed to be their governor in the land of Judah, from the twentieth year even unto the two and thirtieth year of Artaxerxes the king, that is, twelve years, I and my brethren have not eaten the bread of the governor. But the former governors that had been before me were chargeable unto the people, and had taken of them bread and wine, beside forty shekels of silver; yea, even their servants bare rule over the people: but so did not I, because of the fear of God. Yea, also I continued in the work of this wall, neither bought we any land: and all my servants were gathered thither unto the work. Moreover there were at my table an hundred and fifty of the Jews and rulers, beside those that came unto us from among the heathen that are about us. Now that which was prepared for me daily was one ox and six choice sheep; also fowls were prepared for me, and once in ten days store of all sorts of wine: yet for all this required not I the bread of the governor, because the bondage was heavy upon this people." – Nehemiah 5:14-18

After a strong rebuke of the nobles and rulers of Jerusalem for fleecing their fellow poor Jews, Nehemiah describes the example he showed them of how leaders should truly act.

Even though Nehemiah and his workers had the right to tax the people of their possessions and money, he chose to not be a burden on them. Rather, he went to the other extreme. He actually provided for himself, his workers, and many others in Jerusalem while he ruled there. Nehemiah recognized that the people were going through a hard time. So, rather than adding to their burden, he wisely chose to help ease their burden. Nehemiah thought of the welfare of others before himself. Perhaps this is why he was such a successful leader!

Whether we are considering politicians, bosses in the workplace, fathers in the home, or leaders in a church; Nehemiah gives an excellent example of how Godly leadership should proceed. Even though a leader may have the *right* to certain privileges and wealth, that does not mean he *has* to take them.

The best leaders throughout history have been willing to suffer with their people and lead them in humbleness. Leaders should always remember that all power and authority on earth still reside under the authority of Jesus Christ.

The Apostle Paul had this testimony to the Elders at Ephesus:

> *"I have coveted no man's silver, or gold, or apparel. Yea, ye yourselves know, that these hands have ministered unto my necessities, and to them that were with me. I have shewed you all things, how that so labouring ye ought to support the weak, and to remember the words of the Lord Jesus, how he said, It is more blessed to give than to receive."*
> *– Acts 20:33-35*

The best way to lead is to lead like Jesus. He led multitudes of people by serving them the things they needed most - grace and truth.

Build your wall...

- Shepherds give comfort by leading. Cattle are driven by coercion and fear. How should we act if we are responsible for others?

- Name or describe someone that led you in a good way and made you feel safe.

- Name or describe someone that used fear or power to make you do something.

25 • I Am Doing a Great Work

"Now it came to pass, when Sanballat, and Tobiah, and Geshem the Arabian, and the rest of our enemies, heard that I had builded the wall, and that there was no breach left therein; (though at that time I had not set up the doors upon the gates;) that Sanballat and Geshem sent unto me, saying, Come, let us meet together in some one of the villages in the plain of Ono. But they thought to do me mischief. And I sent messengers unto them, saying, I am doing a great work, so that I cannot come down: why should the work cease, whilst I leave it, and come down to you? Yet they sent unto me four times after this sort; and I answered them after the same manner." – Nehemiah 6:1-4

Nehemiah had been blessed time and again to lead the Israelites through trials, arguments, and threats. Their work was continuing at an amazing speed. The wall was almost finished. All they had left was to put up the gates and doors.

When Sanballat and the others heard about the progress, they just couldn't stand it. They had tried all their bully tactics and lies, but nothing was slowing down Nehemiah. Other than a full-out attack, they had only one option left: distraction. If they could not get Nehemiah to quit out of fear, perhaps they could distract him so that his work would never be finished.

But, like Bunyun's character in <u>The Pilgrim's Progress</u>, Nehemiah stops his ears to the distraction. He reminds himself and others that the work they are doing is not only good, it is great! It was a huge undertaking, and no distraction should be allowed to get in the way. Nehemiah knew that the very ones who were trying to distract him necessitated the building of the wall!

We too should have this singular focus in our discipleship. We are doing good things as part of a great work! We have the duty of promoting the kingdom of God in our lives and the lives of others all for the glory of God. This is a great work! Let's not allow the distractions of entertainment, laziness, greed, pride, or fame distract us from our work. Why should we turn aside from our great work? The Christian lives which we build are actually saving us from getting caught up in these sins.

Walking like Christ is a great work.

Raising our children in the nurture and admonition of the Lord is a great work.

Reading our Bibles and going to church are great works.

Putting the Lord and His church first in our lives is a great work!

Everything else is a distraction!

As we journey on each day, let us keep in mind the words of this old hymn, "Palms of Victory":

> *"The songsters in the arbor, that stood beside the way*
> *Attracted his attention, inviting his delay*
> *His watchword being 'Onward!', he stopped his ears and ran*
> *Still shouting as he journeyed, 'Deliverance will come!'*
> *Then palms of victory, crowns of glory;*
> *Palms of victory, I shall wear."*

Build your wall...

- What can we do to avoid or ignore distractions to our discipleship?

- How can we recognize that we are doing a good work for the Lord?

- If we are doing a good work for the Lord, how do we tell others without being arrogant?

26 • Don't Believe Everything You Hear

"Then sent Sanballat his servant unto me in like manner the fifth time with an open letter in his hand; wherein was written, It is reported among the heathen, and Gashmu saith it, that thou and the Jews think to rebel: for which cause thou buildest the wall, that thou mayest be their king, according to these words. And thou hast also appointed prophets to preach of thee at Jerusalem, saying, There is a king in Judah: and now shall it be reported to the king according to these words. Come now therefore, and let us take counsel together. Then I sent unto him, saying, There are no such things done as thou sayest, but thou feignest them out of thine own heart. For they all made us afraid, saying, Their hands shall be weakened from the work, that it be not done. Now therefore, O God, strengthen my hands."

— Nehemiah 6:5-9

After several attempts to pull Nehemiah away from the work with distracting offers, Sanballat sends a letter to Nehemiah that is full of lies and rumors. His hope is to, once again, distract Nehemiah from his work to spend time dealing with these false allegations. The rumors, no doubt, are hurtful. They accuse Nehemiah of doing things against the king and for his own glory. If Sanballat is able to convince the Israelites that Nehemiah simply has plans for personal power and glory, then they will become discouraged and stop working.

The "open letter" is an important thing to recognize in Sanballat's allegations. Normally, letters between leaders are sealed for private discussion. Sanballat sends an open letter so that everyone can hear the allegations against Nehemiah even before Nehemiah does. When Sanballat says there are rumors among the heathen that Nehemiah is doing something wrong, he is not lying. There were rumors, and Sanballat had started them with this open letter! You may notice that many times when someone falsely accuses another, the accuser is guilty of the very same thing!

Rather than getting bogged down in the allegations, Nehemiah flat out refutes them and continues living a life showing the rumors were all lies. He recognizes that this is Sanballat's attempt to discourage him and slow down the work. Therefore, he, once again, prays to God, and then gets back to work!

The enemies of God and His people will do anything they can to bring us down, mock us, and hamper our efforts to glorify God in this world. People are going to make up stories and tell rumors. There is nothing you can do to stop them, and it is a wasted effort to try and fix everything they mess up. When you try to live a righteous life, you may especially become a target of ridicule. The best thing to do is to live above all reproach. Let your life be a shining example so that when rumors pop up, no one will believe them.

> *"Having a good conscience; that, whereas they speak evil of you, as of evildoers, they may be ashamed that falsely accuse your good conversation in Christ." – 1st Peter 3:16*

Build your wall...

⚒ What should we do if we hear a rumor about someone else?

⚒ Some people make up things about us and spread lies about us. What should we do when this happens?

27 • Try the Spirits

"Afterward I came unto the house of Shemaiah the son of Delaiah the son of Mehetabeel, who was shut up; and he said, Let us meet together in the house of God, within the temple, and let us shut the doors of the temple: for they will come to slay thee; yea, in the night will they come to slay thee. And I said, Should such a man as I flee? and who is there, that, being as I am, would go into the temple to save his life? I will not go in. And, lo, I perceived that God had not sent him; but that he pronounced this prophecy against me: for Tobiah and Sanballat had hired him. Therefore was he hired, that I should be afraid, and do so, and sin, and that they might have matter for an evil report, that they might reproach me. My God, think thou upon Tobiah and Sanballat according to these their works, and on the prophetess Noadiah, and the rest of the prophets, that would have put me in fear."
– Nehemiah 6:10-14

After failing to stop Nehemiah's progress with a threat to his reputation, Sanballat and his cohorts devise a plan to cause Nehemiah to fear for his life. They send a false prophet, named Shemaiah, who tries to convince Nehemiah that assassins are going to come kill him during the night. His only safety would be to hide himself in the temple. Ultimately, what they would like to do is make

Nehemiah look like a coward by hiding in the temple when others are still outside. Nehemiah would also violate the law of God by entering into the temple where only priests were allowed.

Nehemiah refuses to go into the temple and hide. He questions why he, a man who has been so greatly blessed thus far by God, would need to run and hide now. The very *idea* of needing to be afraid now proved that this was a false prophet. Nehemiah used simple logical reasoning to deduce the plot of his enemies. He then prayed to God, put it in His hands, and went back to work!

Shemaiah betrayed himself by suggesting things that were contrary to God's direct instruction. He told Nehemiah to hide in the temple where only priests are allowed to go. A true prophet or teacher will *never* tell you to do something that is contrary to the revealed will of God in scripture. Secondly, Shemaiah attempted to cause Nehemiah to doubt about the care and providence of God. God had mightily delivered him to this point: why should Nehemiah all of the sudden need to be afraid? True men of God bring a message of *comfort* to the people of God, not warnings and threats (Isaiah 40:1).

There are many valuable lessons that we can learn from this small portion of scripture, not the least of which is how to recognize a false prophet! In our daily growth in discipleship, there will be many people that will offer us quick helps or new ways to discover more about God. We need to be as vigilant as Nehemiah when this happens and recognize what is going on. True wisdom only comes through diligent study, prayer, and application of the scriptures in our daily walk.

> *"Beloved, believe not every spirit, but try the spirits whether they are*
> *of God: because many false prophets are gone out into the world."*

> *– 1 John 4:1*

In this verse, the Apostle John is telling us to examine the sources and nature of influences on us. The best way to tell whether advice or counsel you receive is godly is to compare it to the word of God, the Bible. If you are familiar with the Bible, true spiritual helpers will simply remind you of the promises of God that you have already learned from scripture. If the words of the *helper* are contrary to the words of God, ignore the *helper* and get back to work! Further, we should consider closely the messages that God sends through His ministers. If it tells us we are out of the way, we need to repent and get back on the narrow path. Those admonitions were sent in love and should not be ignored!

Build your wall...

> ⚒ Will God ever tell us to do something that is contrary to His written word in the Bible?

> ⚒ How can we tell if something that is trying to influence is godly or not?

28 • Wow, That Was Fast!

"So the wall was finished in the twenty and fifth day of the month Elul, in fifty and two days. And it came to pass, that when all our enemies heard thereof, and all the heathen that were about us saw these things, they were much cast down in their own eyes: for they perceived that this work was wrought of our God. Moreover in those days the nobles of Judah sent many letters unto Tobiah, and the letters of Tobiah came unto them. For there were many in Judah sworn unto him, because he was the son in law of Shechaniah the son of Arah; and his son Johanan had taken the daughter of Meshullam the son of Berechiah. Also they reported his good deeds before me, and uttered my words to him. And Tobiah sent letters to put me in fear." – Nehemiah 6:15-19

Despite all the efforts of the enemies of Israel, the walls of Jerusalem were completed in a record-breaking matter of time, just 52 days! It is amazing what can be accomplished when the people of God work together and trust the Lord.

However, we can also see from this lesson that the struggle against evil is not over when our defense has been made. Tobiah *was* ashamed, but that enraged him all the more against Nehemiah. He continued his evil alliances with the nobles inside Jerusalem who fed him information. Tobiah also used a marriage into one of the major builder's families, Meshullam, to try to gain more intelligence about Nehemiah through spying.

Nehemiah wisely ignores all these wicked influences and distractions. His enemies were very busy trying to bring him down, but Nehemiah just stayed the course. Eventually, Tobiah sees all his plans are not getting him the intelligence he needs to defeat Nehemiah, so he just fires off another threatening letter.

Scoffers may mock your work as a Christian, but continue on in prayer and duty. For what you will find is that, when God uses you in a mighty way, the scoffer shames himself and must admit that God has blessed you!

Also, surround yourself with wise counsel. Fellow Bible students are the best help in making decisions. Finally, beware of spies. The devil is not going to attack head on when he can infiltrate your life without your knowledge.

With a hammer in one hand and a sword in the other, "build up" and "fight on," good brother!

Build your wall...

- If we are doing the right thing for the right reasons, are we responsible for how others see it and react?

- If you were to time how long things influence you throughout the week, how would things outside the church compare to time spent in church and fellowship?

29 • Can I Trust You?

"Now it came to pass, when the wall was built, and I had set up the doors, and the porters and the singers and the Levites were appointed, that I gave my brother Hanani, and Hananiah the ruler of the palace, charge over Jerusalem: for he was a faithful man, and feared God above many. And I said unto them, Let not the gates of Jerusalem be opened until the sun be hot; and while they stand by, let them shut the doors, and bar them: and appoint watches of the inhabitants of Jerusalem, every one in his watch, and every one to be over against his house." – Nehemiah 7:1-3

Having reliable friends and brethren is truly a blessing from God. But how do you know whom you can trust? That is an important question.

The work to rebuild the wall was now finished, and the work in the temple had begun once again. Therefore, Nehemiah made ready to go back to Persia to give a report to Artaxerxes. He felt comfortable leaving because he had men that he trusted who could hold leadership until he returned.

This was not a blind trust. Hanani was the brother who first gave the report of the condition of Jerusalem to Nehemiah in Chapter 1. He had been fully invested in the work from the very beginning. Hananiah had also been diligent in the work to rebuild the walls. Nehemiah trusted these two men to rule in his place while he was gone.

Nehemiah gave these men explicit instructions for the defense of the city. Before leaving, he reminded all those in charge to understand the importance of filling their roles so the city would be safe. He made it very clear that only those who were part of the effort were to be in charge of security, and no outsiders were to be hired to help keep the city safe.

Nehemiah's example tells us that we can trust people based on our experiences with them. You should not have to ask someone if you can trust them. Their behavior in past experiences with you should be the proof.

Integrity must be proven before trust can be bestowed. As we have seen several times in previous lessons, when we are faithful in the little things, we are faithful in much. We cannot claim that we will be faithful to handle larger responsibilities if we have not done our daily labors in the Lord.

Another important aspect of this account relates to our church experience. Only those who have been actively involved in activities should have influential roles. The lazy nobles were not trusted with leadership because they had not proven themselves. Just because they have money does not mean they have spiritual maturity. Also, no outsiders were allowed to defend the city. The care of our church congregations should be very *personal* in nature. We can only love and protect those that we know well. That kind of care cannot be hired out to counselors or motivational trainers.

The Lord will raise up gifts within the church to care for it.

Build your wall...

- If someone says, "You can trust me," can you trust them?

- Should we need to add the words "I promise" or "I swear" when we make statements?

- How do we develop integrity?

30 • Census Report

Please read Nehemiah 7:4-73

The remainder of chapter seven contains a lengthy census of Jews and a few details about donations for the restarting of temple worship and sacrifice. If you are like me, when I read a genealogy like this one in Nehemiah, my brain drifts very quickly. About halfway through the list, I start hearing the teacher from the old Peanuts cartoons, "Wah wah wah wah wah." Or, to be honest, sometimes I have skipped the lists altogether. Then one day, I remembered, "All scripture is given by inspiration of God." That includes these genealogies. I may not understand the purpose for it now, but I may need it later.

Truthfully, I am not fully convinced in my mind why the Holy Spirit would have Nehemiah give these lists here, but if I might, I would like to offer a few possibilities. And with those possibilities, I would like to make some practical application for our personal discipleship and church order.

First of all, you will notice that there were a large number of people that were involved in the work but did not build or rebuild houses inside the walls of Jerusalem. One of the main reasons for the genealogies may be for safety and accountability. The governor of an area needs to know who he governs so that he can keep them safe and maintain a rule of law. I think this aspect is absolutely vital for a healthy New Testament church. Complete anonymity of a person in a church is foreign to the new testament pattern. The congregants knew one another and the pastor and deacons were truly able to help those with spiritual and physical needs because they knew the person not just the name!

Along this same line of reasoning is the accountability issue. Nehemiah saw that it would be better for the city if families who had houses lying in ruins inside the wall would come and rebuild. This focus on the city rather than just individual families has a direct correlation to church. A church cannot thrive if its members do *some* work for the church but are not wholly invested in the growth of the body of Christ. Again, an accurate membership list will help in this area. But please understand, I am not talking about a list of known donors! Churches should never think that way. I am talking about the spiritual participation of membership.

Another possible reason for the inclusion of such a list here is honor and respect. The list is not to be used to make someone famous but to be able to point to them as good examples who deserve respect of others that come later. The church should never revere its older or past members as a higher order of saints. We are all saints in Christ. However, a healthy amount of respect for the work of those that the Lord used to start a church or to get it through rough times ought to be given.

The third possibility, and probably the main reason for the inclusion that I can see, is that it most likely adds to the evidence of the genealogies of Jesus Christ. These lists add credibility to the lists provided by Matthew and Luke in their gospel accounts.

Build your wall...

- If you would receive nothing in return or benefit from doing a good work, would you do it anyway?

- If you were your church's best member, what kind of church would you have? Be honest! (This can also relate to family.)

31 • How Long Was That Sermon?

"And all the people gathered themselves together as one man into the street that was before the water gate; and they spake unto Ezra the scribe to bring the book of the law of Moses, which the Lord had commanded to Israel." – Nehemiah 8:1

After the miraculous rebuilding effort of the walls of Jerusalem, the people were so strongly unified that Nehemiah says that they were as "one man." It is amazing how hard work and trial will bring people together.

Even more amazing was the *cause* for their gathering. They were gathered together for church and were prompting Ezra to get out a Bible and preach to them. This was nothing like what we see so often today, where men of God are being blessed to preach the gospel in power, but they preach to half-empty buildings. No leader forced these people to come together and listen against their will. The people felt the blessing of God on them in their work, and now they wanted to worship!

Do we lack zeal in our worship today? Is this idea of unity foreign to us? Perhaps it is because we have lived too comfortably for too long. Perhaps we need to seek the benefit of the kingdom of God (our home church) more than our own personal pleasure or peace. Perhaps we need to realize that the spiritual walls in our lives need some rebuilding work. We may be in danger and just not see it because we are blinded by worldly comforts. Or perhaps, we have made allies with the world like the arrogant nobles did with Sanballat and Tobiah.

The people came together in a "grand homecoming" for the benefit of one another and, more importantly, for the glory of God. The result was a strong desire to devote themselves to God in worship. This is the result of having vested interest in the kingdom!

> *And Ezra the priest brought the law before the congregation both of men and women, and all that could hear with understanding, upon the first day of the seventh month. And he read therein before the street that was before the water gate from the morning until midday, before the men and the women, and those that could understand; and the ears of all the people were attentive unto the book of the law. And Ezra the scribe stood upon a pulpit of wood, which they had made for the purpose; and beside him stood Mattithiah, and Shema, and Anaiah, and Urijah, and Hilkiah, and Maaseiah, on his right hand; and on his left hand, Pedaiah, and Mishael, and Malchiah, and Hashum, and Hashbadana, Zechariah, and Meshullam. And Ezra opened the book in the sight of all the people; (for he was above all the people;) and when he opened it, all the people stood up: and Ezra blessed the Lord, the great God. And all the people answered, Amen, Amen, with lifting up their hands: and they bowed their heads, and worshipped the Lord with their faces to the ground. Also Jeshua, and Bani, and Sherebiah, Jamin, Akkub, Shabbethai, Hodijah, Maaseiah, Kelita, Azariah, Jozabad, Hanan, Pelaiah, and the Levites, caused the people to understand the law: and the people stood in their place. So they read in the book in the law of God distinctly, and gave the sense, and caused them to understand the reading. – Nehemiah 8:2-8*

In the typical "corporate church" on Sunday, you might hear a discourse that is 15 to 20 minutes long. The message may or may not use the Bible for its anchor. The speaker might not even quote a single scripture to support his message. Unfortunately, most of these *worship* services are little more than a rock/pop concert that includes a little motivational speech somewhere in the middle. The Bible takes a secondary role if it is used at all.

Here in Nehemiah, Chapter 8, we find a remarkable event. Verse one showed us that it was the *people* who were eager to hear the word of God, not just the preachers. Nehemiah tells us that Ezra read from the word of God, and he and the other Levites preached for about six hours! Not only that, the people stood the entire time shouting "amen," lifting up their hands, and bowing down their heads! This was a great revival, and it was ALL PREACHING!

Here are a few other things of note in this great revival service:

- There were *not* several different services. They found a way for everyone to worship together as families.
- No one complained about the time. They devoted themselves to worship and nothing else.
- The content of the messages was completely scripture related. They gave expository delivery of the word of God and then explained what each verse meant.

Some might say, "Well, that was then. The New Testament worship looked nothing like that." Wrong. It looked exactly like this, long sermons and all. As a matter of fact, the Lord typically blessed the congregation abundantly when they met in such a manner!

> *"And upon the first day of the week, when the disciples came together to break bread, Paul preached unto them, ready to depart on the morrow; and continued his speech until midnight. And there were many lights in the upper chamber, where they were gathered together. And there sat in a window a certain young man named Eutychus, being fallen into a deep sleep: and as Paul was long preaching, he sunk down with sleep, and fell down from the third loft, and was taken up dead. And Paul went down, and fell on him, and embracing him said, Trouble not yourselves; for his life is in him. When he therefore was come up again, and had broken bread, and eaten, and talked a long while, even till break of day, so he departed. And they brought the young man alive, and were not a little comforted." – Acts 20:7-12*

In an effort to increase congregation size, I fear many have moved away from this Biblical model to the entertainment model. Perhaps instead of a concert, the people of God need to rebuild the walls of their lives in repentance so that they may desire to hear good preaching and be blessed with *true* revival in their worship.

Build your wall...

⚒. How long is the typical sermon you hear on Sunday?

⚒. How much scripture is used in that sermon?

⚒. Is it reasonable to ask you pastor to preach more Bible if you are not willing to read it more?

32 • Let's Go Eat!

"And Nehemiah, which is the Tirshatha, and Ezra the priest the scribe, and the Levites that taught the people, said unto all the people, This day is holy unto the Lord your God; mourn not, nor weep. For all the people wept, when they heard the words of the law. Then he said unto them, Go your way, eat the fat, and drink the sweet, and send portions unto them for whom nothing is prepared: for this day is holy unto our Lord: neither be ye sorry; for the joy of the Lord is your strength. So the Levites stilled all the people, saying, Hold your peace, for the day is holy; neither be ye grieved. And all the people went their way to eat, and to drink, and to send portions, and to make great mirth, because they had understood the words that were declared unto them." – Nehemiah. 8:9-12

Upon hearing the word of God preached to them for the first time in a very long time, the people felt convicted of their sin of neglect of the law and other sins as well. The people had asked Ezra to teach them. They had listened to six hours of preaching, and now they were full of sorrow for their sin.

Ezra, recognizing this true sorrow for sin, could see that the people were repenting of their ways and were now spiritually ready to be taught the word of

God more deeply. Knowing that to commit their lives to God's service is a great effort, and that they had been standing for six hours, Ezra tells the people to go home and refresh themselves. But his command was not just to go home for a simple meal. He wants them to have a feast of the best that they have. They are also to send food and drink to the poor among them so that everyone could enjoy the feast. This feast was to remind the people of the mercy of God toward Israel. Their repentance was not the cause of the mercy of God. It was evidence that God had already had mercy on them and blessed them to see their sin so they could repent. It was then fitting for them to have a feast in the liberty of the mercy of God.

Most *corporate* worship services look nothing like this event or anything like the first century church for that matter. The message from mainstream pulpits today is basically a feel-good, motivational message telling the people what God wants to do for them with material blessings if they will just let Him. There is no moral absolute described and therefore, no sorrow for sin. This kind of "worship" breeds congregants that are eager for the feast but see no need for repentance to precede the celebration. They just want the party. If the message does not encourage transforming your life to be more like Christ, then it is a message that encourages you to be comfortable where you are and continue to conform to the world. This is not the gospel.

Our church service today should look much like this event in Nehemiah which is strikingly similar to the first century church. The focus should not be entertainment, but a prompting to holiness and following Jesus. I believe one of the most concise instructions for preachers of all generations can be found in Isaiah, Chapter 40. There we read that the message to the people of God should be one of "double" comfort.

> *"Comfort ye, comfort ye my people, saith your God. Speak ye comfortably to Jerusalem, and cry unto her, that her warfare is accomplished, that her iniquity is pardoned: for she hath received of the Lord's hand double for all her sins." – Isaiah 40:1-2*

Before you jump to the conclusion that the preacher's message should make people feel "comfortable" where they are at, continue reading. We find that the first part of the message of comfort is to tell people their condition without the grace of God. "All flesh is grass" is a statement of complete depravity. When people see their sinful condition, they will mourn, but they will also see the need of a Savior! Only the child of God, who has truly seen his sin, can truly rejoice in the double blessing of mercy and grace.

Once that true repentance is felt, the feast of liberty in Christ should come forth in the way the person lives. Once they see that without Christ they are nothing, they can fully understand that they have everything they need in Christ. Their salvation is not based upon their works or will. They can lay aside that burden and take up the yoke of mercy and grace. They can go and have a feast of the best blessings of God and share it in love with all those around them.

Build your wall...

- Have you mourned for your sin and the sins of others while in worship?

- Are you more entertained by certain preaching styles than others?

- What can you do to worship more like the New Testament demonstrates?

33 • Bible Study

*"And on the second day were gathered together the chief of the fathers
of all the people, the priests, and the Levites, unto Ezra the scribe, even
to understand the words of the law." – Nehemiah 8:13*

The entire congregation met the day before in formal worship. On this occasion,
a smaller group meets in order to *understand* a part of the law.

Whether it is a preachers' meeting, an organized church meeting, or an informal
meeting in your home; when you meet to *understand* the word of God, you are
having a Bible study.

And this is a good thing!

Consider this:

*"These were more noble than those in Thessalonica, in that they
received the word with all readiness of mind, and searched the
scriptures daily, whether those things were so." – Acts 17:11*

Now, the brethren at Thessalonica were not slackers concerning their devotion. They endured a lot of persecution during Paul's visit and no doubt afterward as well. Paul even says the manner in which they received the gospel in such conditions was an evidence of their election by God (1st Thessalonians 1:4)!

However, Luke records that the brethren at Berea were more noble. On what criteria did he base this conclusion? Their amount of Bible study.

Our discipleship is not just attending a worship service and a few other activities. To be disciples we must truly be learning the discipline of the life of Christ. This cannot be accomplished in only an hour or so on Sunday morning. I, personally, cannot see how a pastor can accomplish the duty of *teaching* the congregation without a time, formal or informal, for congregants to ask questions and gain clarification.

Asking a preacher a question and "questioning" a preacher are not the same thing. We all (including preachers) need to realize we don't know everything there is to know about our Wonderful Savior. Therefore, we should all be good Bible students in formal worship, in personal study, in family fellowship, and in Bible study whenever possible.

Build your wall...

- Is it ok to ask a preacher questions? What if he will not take questions?

- If the preacher preaches the Bible correctly, and we do not like it, what should we do?

34 • Let's Go Camping

"And they found written in the law which the Lord had commanded by Moses, that the children of Israel should dwell in booths in the feast of the seventh month: and that they should publish and proclaim in all their cities, and in Jerusalem, saying, Go forth unto the mount, and fetch olive branches, and pine branches, and myrtle branches, and palm branches, and branches of thick trees, to make booths, as it is written. So the people went forth, and brought them, and made themselves booths, every one upon the roof of his house, and in their courts, and in the courts of the house of God, and in the street of the water gate, and in the street of the gate of Ephraim. And all the congregation of them that were come again out of the captivity made booths, and sat under the booths: for since the days of Jeshua the son of Nun unto that day had not the children of Israel done so. And there was very great gladness. Also day by day, from the first day unto the last day, he read in the book of the law of God. And they kept the feast seven days; and on the eighth day was a solemn assembly, according unto the manner." – Nehemiah 8:14-18

The study of the law revealed to the leaders and the priests that there was a festival fast approaching that they were to observe. This "Feast of Tabernacles" was to remind the Jews of the forty years they dwelt in the desert after God had delivered them from Egyptian bondage. Along with the other things that attended Jewish celebrations, the people were to make tents out of branches and sleep in their yards throughout the entire week.

It is very important to see that this symbol was the only symbol given by God to remember their time in the wilderness. God is the Creator. He knows how the mind of His creation operates. Therefore, He knows what the best symbol is to help His children remember, and He said they should sleep in tents.

It is also exciting to note that Jesus was born in late September or early October just after this festival. John records in John 1:14, that the "Word was made flesh and *dwelt* among us." The Greek word for *dwelt* in this verse is also tent or tabernacle! God was with the natural Israelites in the wilderness, and Jesus dwelt among God's children during His time here on earth.

There are many ceremonies, sacrifices, and observances in the Old Testament Law that are not necessary to observe today. These things were pointing toward Christ. Christ fulfilled the pictures in these symbols, therefore the symbols are no longer needed. There are symbols of observance given in the New Testament, but *very* few. These, then, must be seen as precious and carefully observed.

Among these New Testament symbols, we find the communion of the Lord's Supper. In this ceremony, unleavened bread and wine are used to symbolize the work of Jesus Christ in His life and on the cross. Jesus told us what the two symbols represent, and He told us to do the ceremony in remembrance of Him.

Jesus never instructed us to adorn ourselves with Christian symbols in jewelry (especially not tattoos!). Nor did He tell us to cover our houses of worship in the artwork of men's hands portraying His suffering. He told us to observe this simple supper.

To say that we remember our Savior better through these other things would be equivalent to a Jew saying, "I don't think I will sleep in a tent this week. I mean, I already wear this tent charm on my necklace all the time."

Other symbols are not evil in and of themselves, but they must not replace or usurp the clear symbol that was given by the Lord!

Build your wall...

✝ Is it ok to substitute what God has told us to do with things that we prefer to do if they are not evil? Explain.

✝ Would others recognize you as disciple of Jesus without any outward symbols in jewelry, artwork in your home, or stickers on your car?

✝ What are we telling others about God if we use symbols to identify us as Christian but then act unlovingly?

35 • True Repentance Revisited

"Now in the twenty and fourth day of this month the children of Israel were assembled with fasting, and with sackclothes, and earth upon them. And the seed of Israel separated themselves from all strangers, and stood and confessed their sins, and the iniquities of their fathers. And they stood up in their place, and read in the book of the law of the Lord their God one fourth part of the day; and another fourth part they confessed, and worshipped the Lord their God."
— Nehemiah 9:1-3

In Chapter 1, we found Nehemiah on his knees in sorrow for the sin of Israel. He did not make excuses for his forefathers, for his brethren, or for himself. He confessed all, threw himself at the feet of the Almighty, and begged for mercy.

We now see the nation of Israel as a whole doing the very same thing.

The celebration was now over and a period of sorrow for sin had begun. The people, having seen in the word of God that they should not have any form of relationship with the strangers around them, cut off all relations with those that would draw them away from their service to God. This is a sure sign of true repentance. Any person may say that they repent and want to do better. It is a true disciple that first casts away all practice of sin and then makes confession of his faults.

We once again find that there is no rush to finish these kinds of devotions. They spent half the day in a service of confession and worship.

Confession and repentance are vital elements that attend proper worship. The worship of God is more than singing, preaching, and praying. These are the tools of worship, but the substance of worship is a sinner who has seen his need for a Savior.

David understood that the true strength of Zion was not just in its walls and worship services. Those elements are only effective when the people see themselves as sinners.

> *"For thou desirest not sacrifice; else would I give it: thou delightest not in burnt offering. The sacrifices of God are a broken spirit: a broken and a contrite heart, O God, thou wilt not despise. Do good in thy good pleasure unto Zion: build thou the walls of Jerusalem. Then shalt thou be pleased with the sacrifices of righteousness, with burnt offering and whole burnt offering: then shall they offer bullocks upon thine altar." – Psalm 51:16-19*

To truly draw nigh to God, we must flee from the sin of the world.

Build your wall...

- What should you do if you have repented of a sin but are committing it again?

- Is God pleased with our behavior if we go through the formality of worship but do nothing to try to live a better life?

36 • The Faithful Mercy of God

"Then stood up upon the stairs, of the Levites, Jeshua, and Bani, Kadmiel, Shebaniah, Bunni, Sherebiah, Bani, and Chenani, and cried with a loud voice unto the Lord their God. Then the Levites, Jeshua, and Kadmiel, Bani, Hashabniah, Sherebiah, Hodijah, Shebaniah, and Pethahiah, said, Stand up and bless the Lord your God for ever and ever: and blessed be thy glorious name, which is exalted above all blessing and praise". – Nehemiah 9:4-5

The sin of Israel was great and so should be the repentance of it. The religious leaders did not shy away but shouted their confessions and need of mercy.

The Levites then turned to those who had fallen on their faces in confession and told them to stand up. They were telling them that God *is* merciful and forgives the penitent sinner. Therefore, they should now shout praises of joy and thankfulness to God.

"If we confess our sins, he is faithful and just to forgive us our sins, and to cleanse us from all unrighteousness." – 1st John 1:9

Thankful songs of praise should never stop pouring from the mouths of the elect of God, for He has blessed them with all spiritual blessings. He has chosen them, sanctified them, and predestinated them to be with Him forever. He did these things, not because of their faithfulness, but for the praise of the glory of His grace (Ephesians 1:3-6)!

Our praise, even in all eternity, will never reach the full honor that is due to His majestic name, but that does not mean we should not try. The Psalmist exhorts us:

> *"Great is the Lord, and greatly to be praised in the city of our God, in the mountain of his holiness." – Psalm 48:1*

> *"Great is Thy faithfulness!" "Great is Thy faithfulness!"*
> *Morning by morning new mercies I see;*
> *All I have needed Thy hand hath provided—*
> *"Great is Thy faithfulness," Lord, unto me!*
>   *–   Thomas O. Chisholm*

Build your wall...

✕ What kind of songs should we sing in worship?

✕ Who should be singing thankful praise to God?

✕ What if I don't sing very well? What do I do?

37 • Historical Foundations for Faith - Part 1

Today we will begin examining a prayer recorded by Nehemiah. The prayer of the Levites was spoken in confession and repentance. It is a brief but awesome history of the power *and* mercy of God. Let us take just a glimpse at some of His glories!

The Levites begin by listing five blessings of God on His creation and people. We will look at three in part one and the other two in the next article.

1. One of the most clear expressions of God's power is His creation of all things.

> *"Thou, even thou, art Lord alone; thou hast made heaven, the heaven of heavens, with all their host, the earth, and all things that are therein, the seas, and all that is therein, and thou preservest them all; and the host of heaven worshippeth thee." – Nehemiah 9:6*

The material universe testifies to the glory and majesty of God.

> *"The heavens declare the glory of God; and the firmament sheweth his handywork." – Psalm 19:1*

If the material things of creation worship God, should not the intelligent beings created in His image do the same?

> *"For by him were all things created, that are in heaven, and that are in earth, visible and invisible, whether they be thrones, or dominions, or principalities, or powers: all things were created by him, and for him:" – Colossians 1:16*

The more man discovers about the universe, the more clear vision we get of the Mighty God!

2. God, in His abundant mercy, chose to bring Abraham out of the false religion of the world and show unto Him the riches that He has for His people.

> *"Thou art the Lord the God, who didst choose Abram, and broughtest him forth out of Ur of the Chaldees, and gavest him the name of Abraham; and foundest his heart faithful before thee, and madest a covenant with him to give the land of the Canaanites, the Hittites, the Amorites, and the Perizzites, and the Jebusites, and the Girgashites, to give it, I say, to his seed, and hast performed thy words; for thou art righteous:" – Nehemiah 9:7-8*

The children of Israel, by God's mercy, were able to return to the very land that God promised to Abraham and to his natural seed. But let us not forget, that these things were spoken to us pointing toward a promise to the Israel of God (Galatians 6:16).

In the Seed of Abraham, which is Jesus Christ (Galatians 3:16), God blesses all of His elect children in every nation (Revelation 5:9).

3. With a mighty hand, God delivered Israel from the hand of Pharaoh in Egypt.

> *"and didst see the affliction of our fathers in Egypt, and heardest their cry by the Red sea; and shewedst signs and wonders upon Pharaoh, and on all his servants, and on all the people of his land: for thou knewest that they dealt proudly against them. So didst thou get thee a name, as it is this day. And thou didst divide the sea before them, so that they went through the midst of the sea on the dry land; and their persecutors thou threwest into the deeps, as a stone into the mighty waters. Moreover thou leddest them in the day by a cloudy pillar; and in the*

night by a pillar of fire, to give them light in the way wherein they should go." – Nehemiah 9:9-12

Egypt clearly resembles bondage in sin. And just as God freed Israel from bondage, He frees His people from the death grip of sin.

> *"For in that he died, he died unto sin once: but in that he liveth, he liveth unto God. Likewise reckon ye also yourselves to be dead indeed unto sin, but alive unto God through Jesus Christ our Lord. Let not sin therefore reign in your mortal body, that ye should obey it in the lusts thereof. Neither yield ye your members as instruments of unrighteousness unto sin: but yield yourselves unto God, as those that are alive from the dead, and your members as instruments of righteousness unto God. For sin shall not have dominion over you: for ye are not under the law, but under grace." – Romans 6:10-14*

God will ultimately save us from the penalty and presence of sin in glory, but He has also saved us from its grip so that we may walk in newness of life here and now.

Build your wall...

⚒. Is it possible to believe what the Bible says and believe in evolution?

⚒. Why should we think of past deliverances by God when we need help?

38 • Historical Foundations for Faith - Part 2

In our previous devotion, we looked at three of the five foundations that Israel had for trusting God in the prayer of the Levites. Today, we will explore the last two.

4. God revealed the full nature of His holiness when He gave the law on Mount Sanai.

> *"Thou camest down also upon mount Sinai, and spakest with them from heaven, and gavest them right judgments, and true laws, good statutes and commandments: and madest known unto them thy holy sabbath, and commandedst them precepts, statutes, and laws, by the hand of Moses thy servant:" – Nehemiah 9:13-14*

God never intended the law to be a recipe on how to get to heaven. The law gives knowledge of sin by comparing our behavior to the holiness of God (Romans 3:20).

However, the law does give us the pattern of holiness that we should seek to copy in our lives. We do this in thankfulness because Jesus Christ *did* fulfill the law. And His righteousness is counted to us by the mercy of God!

5. God provided for the daily needs of His people in the wilderness.

> *"and gavest them bread from heaven for their hunger, and broughtest forth water for them out of the rock for their thirst, and promisedst them that they should go in to possess the land which thou hadst sworn to give them." – Nehemiah 9:15*

God will not forsake the physical or spiritual needs of His people (Matthew 6:33).

We have Jesus' own words telling us that He is the source of life for us just like He was for Israel in the wilderness.

> *"I am that bread of life. Your fathers did eat manna in the wilderness, and are dead. This is the bread which cometh down from heaven, that a man may eat thereof, and not die. I am the living bread which came down from heaven: if any man eat of this bread, he shall live for ever: and the bread that I will give is my flesh, which I will give for the life of the world." – John 6:48-51*

And Paul tells us:

> *"And did all drink the same spiritual drink: for they drank of that spiritual Rock that followed them: and that Rock was Christ." – 1st Corinthians 10:4*

We do not have to blindly take a leap of faith in order to trust God. That concept is foreign to the Bible. We may not understand everything, and that is why we need faith to trust God. However, we also have the word of God showing us *why* we should trust Him. We should trust Him because He is faithful to Himself and has promised Himself that He would have mercy on us and save us.

Build your wall...

🔨 What do you say to someone who tells you to take a leap of faith?

🔨 Does faith trust our "ability to continue in faith" or does it simply "trust God"?

39 • God's Response to Our Pride

"But they and our fathers dealt proudly, and hardened their necks, and hearkened not to thy commandments, and refused to obey, neither were mindful of thy wonders that thou didst among them; but hardened their necks, and in their rebellion appointed a captain to return to their bondage: but thou art a God ready to pardon, gracious and merciful, slow to anger, and of great kindness, and forsookest them not." – Nehemiah 9:16-17

God had been abundantly merciful to Israel in delivering them out of bondage in Egypt, but they answered that blessing with pride and sin. They were willing to return to slavery rather than follow the will of God Who had delivered them. They forgot, or ignored, the miracles of the Red Sea, the manna, the water from the rock, and the other wondrous things God had done for them. In their pride, they lost their rational minds! God was blessing them, but they were choosing slavery under a defeated king rather than service to an all-powerful and merciful God.

But how did God answer? In wrath? No.

Nehemiah reminds us that God is not eager to seek vengeance upon His people. He is *ready* to pardon. He is full of grace and mercy. He is actually *slow* to anger. And, as Jesus said, He will never leave His children nor forsake them.

If we truthfully consider the pattern of our own lives, we must all admit that we act just like the Israelites at times. We are happy with what we are doing and don't want to change! We should rightly expect a Holy God to wipe us out for our un-thankfulness and pride. And yet, He shows mercy and pardon instead.

This should move our hearts to seek His will and love Him all the more. He has granted mercy and not vengeance. He has given grace and lifted us to heavenly places in Christ. He has chosen us by His sovereign will and will bring us to Himself at the end of time.

Let us consider the actions of the Israelites as an example of what *not* to do when we sin and God still has mercy. Instead, let us live a life of joyful thankfulness in obedience to His will.

Build your wall...

⚒ Do Christians have a reason to brag because they followed Christ?

⚒ Are we allowed to think ourselves better than someone else because we followed Christ?

40 • Folded Pieces of Paper

"Yea, when they had made them a molten calf, and said, This is thy God that brought thee up out of Egypt, and had wrought great provocations; yet thou in thy manifold mercies forsookest them not in the wilderness: the pillar of the cloud departed not from them by day, to lead them in the way; neither the pillar of fire by night, to shew them light, and the way wherein they should go. Thou gavest also thy good spirit to instruct them, and withheldest not thy manna from their mouth, and gavest them water for their thirst. Yea, forty years didst thou sustain them in the wilderness, so that they lacked nothing; their clothes waxed not old, and their feet swelled not."

– Nehemiah 9:18-21

The pride of the Israelites became so great that they created a replacement for the God Who had delivered them!

This may sound so horrible that you would never consider doing this. However, we do this every time we put something before our service to God. Nehemiah shows, in detail, how God responded to offense after offense with *manifold* mercy.

When my daughter, Gracie (the artist for this book) was little, she used to love playing with little bitty toys, trinkets, and pieces of paper. One of her favorite things to do was to see how many times she could fold up a piece of paper so she could fit it into her pocket. My wife and I used to find countless numbers of pieces of paper in her pockets and in the laundry. It was amazing to unfold these papers that were so tiny because with each opening, the paper would double in size until we found it to be an entire piece of notebook paper!

And so it is with the blessing of mercy from God. We see His merciful hand in our lives at times and we think, "Well, isn't that a nice blessing." But then we begin to consider our sin. We see that mercy covered that sin as well. The paper of mercy unfolds.

We look back over our lives at the times we weren't interested in serving the Lord at all. The paper of mercy unfolds before us again.

We can see from God's word that we were even born sinners by nature. The paper of mercy unfolds again.

If we unfold that paper enough times, we will begin to get just a glimpse of the mercy that God has had upon us. I say it is only a glimpse because His mercy toward His children is just as infinite as He is.

> *"The voice of joy, and the voice of gladness, the voice of the bridegroom, and the voice of the bride, the voice of them that shall say, Praise the LORD of hosts: for the LORD is good; for his **mercy endureth for ever**: and of them that shall bring the sacrifice of praise into the house of the LORD. For I will cause to return the captivity of the land, as at the first, saith the LORD." – Jeremiah 33:11*

Build your wall...

✗ Describe an unfolding blessing of God in your life.

✗ Is hearing about blessings in the Bible and God's blessings of others enough for us to find peace? Explain.

41 • Nevertheless – The Cycle Continues

"Moreover thou gavest them kingdoms and nations, and didst divide them into corners: so they possessed the land of Sihon, and the land of the king of Heshbon, and the land of Og king of Bashan. Their children also multipliedst thou as the stars of heaven, and broughtest them into the land, concerning which thou hadst promised to their fathers, that they should go in to possess it. So the children went in and possessed the land, and thou subduedst before them the inhabitants of the land, the Canaanites, and gavest them into their hands, with their kings, and the people of the land, that they might do with them as they would. And they took strong cities, and a fat land, and possessed houses full of all goods, wells digged, vineyards, and oliveyards, and fruit trees in abundance: so they did eat, and were filled, and became fat, and delighted themselves in thy great goodness. Nevertheless they were disobedient, and rebelled against thee, and cast thy law behind their backs, and slew thy prophets which testified against them to turn them to thee, and they wrought great provocations. Therefore thou deliveredst them into the hand of their enemies, who vexed them: and in the time of their trouble, when they cried unto thee, thou heardest them from heaven; and according to thy manifold mercies thou gavest them saviours, who saved them out of the hand of their enemies."

– Nehemiah 9:22-27

God truly blessed His chosen people, Israel.

He providentially guided them to defeat armies, tear down walls of cities, and occupy the promised land of Canaan. They took possession of houses they had not built and ate from crops that they did not plant. Not only that, God took that tiny number that went into Egypt over 400 years before and blessed them to be multiplied beyond number, just as He promised to Abraham. The mercy of God poured out in great measure.

Nevertheless...

The Israelites rebelled against God. Not only did they ignore the law of God, they threw it away like trash and killed the prophets God had sent to guide and instruct them.

As any good father would, God chastised the children of Israel. He did not obliterate them, but neither did He passively ignore their sin. The Israelites, without the blessing of God, were unable to continue to defeat their enemies round about them.

In their pain, the children of Israel cried out, and God answered. Once again the manifold mercy of God was shown, and He sent leaders to guide them against their enemies and back to paths of righteousness.

It cannot be denied that the children of Israel are a picture of the children of God. It also cannot be denied that we so often act just like they did. We are blessed by God with abundance and peace. Then, we get complacent and forget the God Who blessed us.

Thankfully, God is a God of mercy toward His people. He knows just the right amount of chastisement needed. And He is ready to show mercy when we cry out for help in repentance.

> *"But after they had rest, they did evil again before thee: therefore leftest thou them in the hand of their enemies, so that they had the dominion over them: yet when they returned, and cried unto thee, thou heardest them from heaven; and many times didst thou deliver them according to thy mercies; and testifiedst against them, that thou mightest bring them again unto thy law: yet they dealt proudly, and hearkened not unto thy commandments, but sinned against thy judgments, (which if a man do, he shall live in them;) and withdrew the shoulder, and hardened their neck, and would not hear. Yet many years didst thou*

forbear them, and testifiedst against them by thy spirit in thy prophets: yet would they not give ear: therefore gavest thou them into the hand of the people of the lands. Nevertheless for thy great mercies' sake thou didst not utterly consume them, nor forsake them; for thou art a gracious and merciful God." – Nehemiah 9:28-31

The Levites continue their prayer reminding themselves, as they speak to God, that their historical pattern of disobedience was a chronic problem. They did not disobey just once or twice over the years. They had a habitual pattern of taking the mercy of God for granted. After receiving blessing from God, they would, time and again, disobey and reject His law and counsel.

So why did God not just wipe them off the face of the earth?

Mercy.

Mercy is not getting what you deserve for bad behavior. They disobeyed. Therefore, they deserved destruction. Instead, they received mercy in the form of chastisement and deliverance, *every time.* And that is the key. There is no end to the mercy of God toward His people!

We need to not make excuses for our sins. We should confess them and take full responsibility. After all, God knows even the thoughts and intents of our hearts. He can tell *before* we lie to Him! But the joy that is found in the gospel is that we are coming to a merciful Father, not a tyrannical judge.

"But we are all as an unclean thing, and all our righteousnesses are as filthy rags; and we all do fade as a leaf; and our iniquities, like the wind, have taken us away." – Isaiah 64:6

BUT

"This I recall to my mind, therefore have I hope. It is of the Lord's mercies that we are not consumed, because his compassions fail not. They are new every morning: great is thy faithfulness."

– Lamentations 3:21-23

Build your wall...

- If you were God, what would you do to the Israelites who time and again returned to sin?

- How do you think God feels about sins that you continue to commit even though Jesus died for them?

42 • Confession Will Set You Free

"Now therefore, our God, the great, the mighty, and the terrible God, who keepest covenant and mercy, let not all the trouble seem little before thee, that hath come upon us, on our kings, on our princes, and on our priests, and on our prophets, and on our fathers, and on all thy people, since the time of the kings of Assyria unto this day. Howbeit thou art just in all that is brought upon us; for thou hast done right, but we have done wickedly: neither have our kings, our princes, our priests, nor our fathers, kept thy law, nor hearkened unto thy commandments and thy testimonies, wherewith thou didst testify against them. For they have not served thee in their kingdom, and in thy great goodness that thou gavest them, and in the large and fat land which thou gavest before them, neither turned they from their wicked works. Behold, we are servants this day, and for the land that thou gavest unto our fathers to eat the fruit thereof and the good thereof, behold, we are servants in it: and it yieldeth much increase unto the kings whom thou hast set over us because of our sins: also they have dominion over our bodies, and over our cattle, at their pleasure, and we are in great distress. And because of all this we make a sure covenant, and write it; and our princes, Levites, and priests, seal unto it." – Nehemiah 9:32-38

The Levites conclude their prayer with a *full* confession and a vow of devotion to God. I cannot stress enough the importance of understanding how holy God truly is. Although we may think we are doing well because we have turned away from a few sins, that does not mean that we *deserve* the blessing of God. If He chooses to bless us, it is because of His manifold mercy, not our righteousness. Consider this:

> *"And Jesus said unto him, Why callest thou me good? there is none good but one, that is, God." – Mark 10:18*

Our best course when we find ourselves out of the way is to turn back to God in *full* confession. He knows all. Therefore, we should confess all. He is the Sovereign God of glory. Therefore, we should submit ourselves to Him as servants. As often as we see the mercy of God in our lives, we should repent of our sins, and dedicate ourselves once again to His service. And remember, we are not bowing in submission in order to live a depressed life. True devotion to the Lord brings joy and delight because He has mercy on those that seek His face.

> *"When we walk with the Lord in the light of his word,*
> *what a glory he sheds on our way!*
> *While we do his good will, he abides with us still,*
> *and with all who will trust and obey."*
>
> *– John H. Sammis*

Rather than seeing the morality of God as a hindrance to our joy, we should realize that it is our faithfulness to Him that brings us true and lasting joy.

There is a children's story written by Steve Björkman called <u>The Flyaway Kite</u>. It is about a kite that was flying high in the sky on a beautiful spring afternoon. The kite decided he wanted to be free. He fought and fought against the string. Finally, he fought hard enough to break the string. He thought, "I'm free from that old string that was preventing me from having fun!" The kite soon tumbled to the ground. The little boy who was flying the kite came over, fixed the broken pieces of the kite, and tied the string to it once again. The boy tossed the kite back up into the sky, and it soared into the beautiful spring sky once again. It was at that moment that the kite realized that the string (and the boy holding it) were not robbing him of joy. The string, under the control of the boy, is what was causing him to fly high in liberty in the sky.

Build your wall...

- If we think living like Christ will be no fun, what does that say about us?

- Our relationship with God is secure in the finished work of Christ, but how does our behavior affect our fellowship with Him?

43 • Following the Leader

Please read Nehemiah 10:1-29

"Repent ye therefore, and be converted, that your sins may be blotted out, when the times of refreshing shall come from the presence of the Lord;" – Acts 3:19

Often, repentance and conversion are taught as the same act. I believe this verse from Acts, Chapter 3 clearly shows that they are related but definitely different responsibilities of the child of God.

The proper following of true repentance, a change in mind, is true conversion, a change in walk or behavior.

True conversion is marked by a separation from the behaviors, fellowship, and customs of this fallen world. When a person has seen his sins, and felt the forgiving hand of God in mercy upon him, a change in life is the proper response. James confirms this when he says:

> *"Yea, a man may say, Thou hast faith, and I have works: shew me thy*
> *faith without thy works, and I will shew thee my faith by my works."*
> *– James 2:18*

In Nehemiah, Chapter 10, we see many clear parallels between the children of Israel and the true Israel of God, His elect. We can equate the personal behaviors of each directly, and see that the focus on worship, the Levites, and the temple parallel to our devotion to God through His church.

Nehemiah begins by listing the names of the spiritual leaders and family leaders who dedicated themselves to God through the oath mentioned at the close of Chapter 9.

You will notice that Ezra is not listed here. Some speculate that he had returned to Babylon at that time or was sick or in some other way hindered from taking part on this particular day. I think there is a more reasonable answer. Ezra had already dedicated himself to God and his service when he returned years before and rebuilt the temple. There was no need to "rededicate" himself because he had never ceased from doing the will of God.

Eliashib is missing from this list as well. He had made deals with Tobiah and perhaps was unwilling to renounce those things. We will see, in Chapter 13, that Eliashib continued his evil dealings with Tobiah. When Nehemiah returns from giving his status report to the king, he discovers what has been going on and further purges the heathen from Jerusalem and cleanses the temple.

We can see in these verses that the people, in general, follow the actions of their leaders. It is not just the words they speak or preach but their actions that mark true leadership. This is a great example of how a father should lead the home and a pastor should lead the church.

Pastors should lead the congregation:

> *"Brethren, be followers together of me, and mark them which walk so*
> *as ye have us for an ensample." – Philippians 3:17*

Fathers should lead the home:

> *"And, ye fathers, provoke not your children to wrath: but bring them*
> *up in the nurture and admonition of the Lord." – Ephesians 6:4*

Build your wall...

✗. Do we need a formal service of rededicating ourselves to God or do we need to just get back to work?

✗. What should we do with those who do not want to follow the Lord and are influencing our families or church?

44 • Discipleship Is in the Details - Part 1

Often, people will make grand statements to follow and dedicate themselves to God or some other cause in a moment of great passion. The mark of true dedication is when the details of what true dedication mean are carried out in that person's life.

Nehemiah lists eight areas of discipleship that the Israelites agreed to reform. We can see clear parallels in our lives as we seek to be disciples of Jesus Christ. Remember, the term Christian means "follower of Christ."

Today's devotional will cover the first five areas. We will look at the last three in the next article.

> *"and that we would not give our daughters unto the people of the land,
> nor take their daughters for our sons:" – Nehemiah 10:30*

Disciples will not be unequally yoked with the people of the world. This is not forbidding interracial marriage today. It is saying it is wrong for a believer to marry an unbeliever or to have regular fellowship with them.

> *"and if the people of the land bring ware or any victuals on the sabbath*
> *day to sell, that we would not buy it of them on the sabbath, or on the*
> *holy day:" – Nehemiah 10:31a*

They will not do business with the heathen on the Sabbath day. This points out that they are given permission to do necessary business on other days, but the Lord's day (now Sunday) is to be dedicated to His worship and our personal rest.

> *"and that we would leave the seventh year," – Nehemiah 10:31b*

"Leave the seventh year" is in regard to planting and harvesting. This would be the year that the poor could gather freely. This *workfare* system is much better than the government welfare state. Under God's design, the poor still had to do the work in order to eat! We can see this law being followed in the book of Ruth when she goes to glean the fields of Boaz.

> *"and the exaction of every debt." – Nehemiah 10:31c*

In the 7th year, all debts are forgiven. This points to the jubilee in the gospel kingdom as well as the joy of our eternal home.

> *"Also we made ordinances for us, to charge ourselves yearly with the*
> *third part of a shekel for the service of the house of our God; for the*
> *shewbread, and for the continual meat offering, and for the continual*
> *burnt offering, of the sabbaths, of the new moons, for the set feasts, and*
> *for the holy things, and for the sin offerings to make an atonement for*
> *Israel, and for all the work of the house of our God. And we cast the*
> *lots among the priests, the Levites, and the people, for the wood*
> *offering, to bring it into the house of our God, after the houses of our*
> *fathers, at times appointed year by year, to burn upon the altar of the*
> *Lord our God, as it is written in the law:" – Nehemiah 10:32-35*

They agreed to regularly support the monetary needs of the Temple worship. Verse 33-34 gives a list of the needs. This giving was in addition to the first fruit offering in verse 35. In our churches today, this is equivalent to helping with the upkeep of the physical building and grounds. This is done not only through financial support but physical labor as well.

Build your wall...

✖ What are some things that Christians should or should not do that are different than the world?

✖ Can we use others as our excuse if we are not following the Lord? Explain.

45 • Discipleship Is in the Details - Part 2

The last three details of dedication continue with the theme of supporting the worship of God with material things. The financial support of our home church is a vital part of our devoted worship to God. Jesus taught many times of the dangers of loving money rather than God. How we handle our finances is one of the most clear indicators of our trust in God and desire to put Him first in our lives.

"and to bring the firstfruits of our ground, and the firstfruits of all fruit of all trees, year by year, unto the house of the Lord: also the firstborn of our sons, and of our cattle, as it is written in the law, and the firstlings of our herds and of our flocks, to bring to the house of our God, unto the priests that minister in the house of our God: and that we should bring the firstfruits of our dough, and our offerings, and the fruit of all manner of trees, of wine and of oil, unto the priests, to the chambers of the house of our God; and the tithes of our ground unto the Levites, that the same Levites might have the tithes in all the cities of our tillage. And the priest the son of Aaron shall be with the Levites, when the Levites take tithes: and the Levites shall bring up the tithe of the tithes unto the house of our God, to the chambers, into the treasure house. For the children of Israel and the children of Levi shall bring

the offering of the corn, of the new wine, and the oil, unto the chambers, where are the vessels of the sanctuary, and the priests that minister, and the porters, and the singers: and we will not forsake the house of our God." – Nehemiah 10:35-39

They gave the best and first of all their income every year. The harvest happened only once, therefore they gave once. This included animals as well. The equivalent concept for us today is this: If you are paid twice a month, you should give twice a month. You give as the Lord provides.

They gave their firstborn sons to the service. The importance of the firstborn in a family is somewhat lost in our modern culture. The concept refers to more than just our physical firstborn. The Bible is teaching us that, what would be our heritage (firstborn), should be dedicated holy unto God. Therefore, this means we are to give our very best to the Lord in every aspect of our lives and let that be our legacy.

They supported the Levites' physical needs. The Levites were not allowed to own land and earn an income that way. They were to dedicate themselves wholly to the service of God and ministry of the people. The people, in turn, would support them financially. I think this aspect is also extremely vital to the health of a church in the 21st century. A man that is divided between support of his family and study of the word will not be able to do either to the best of his ability.

The last verse points out that the people didn't see this as paying the preacher. They felt if they did not do these things, they were forsaking the house of God.

Two New Testament scriptures come to mind regarding our devotion and quality of discipleship.

"I therefore, the prisoner of the Lord, beseech you that ye walk worthy of the vocation wherewith ye are called," – Ephesians 4:1

"Wherefore gird up the loins of your mind, be sober, and hope to the end for the grace that is to be brought unto you at the revelation of Jesus Christ; as obedient children, not fashioning yourselves according to the former lusts in your ignorance: but as he which hath called you is holy, so be ye holy in all manner of conversation; because it is written, Be ye holy; for I am holy." – 1st Peter 1:13-16

Build your wall...

⚒ Is planned giving to the church faithless giving? Explain.

⚒ Is it wrong for a pastor to be a fulltime minister of the gospel? Explain.

⚒ Is giving to the church just paying the preacher? Explain.

46 • Devotion: Are You Willing or Forced?

"And the rulers of the people dwelt at Jerusalem: the rest of the people also cast lots, to bring one of ten to dwell in Jerusalem the holy city, and nine parts to dwell in other cities. And the people blessed all the men, that willingly offered themselves to dwell at Jerusalem." – Nehemiah 11:1-2

I remember a story about a deacon in a church many years ago. He had lived a pretty rough life to say the least. But after The Lord worked on him, he desired nothing more than to be close to the church and the people of God. The church had to relocate to different meeting houses over the years. Each time the church moved, this faithful deacon would sell his house and move close to the new meeting house location.

Many people considered this an honorable thing to do, and many still hold this as a precious memory. However, not many followed his example.

Nehemiah, Chapter 11 gives details of the repopulation of the city of Jerusalem after the wall was finished. Most of the people had taken part in the rebuilding effort and dedicated themselves to the law of God. However, there were only a few who voluntarily gave up the comforts of living in the outlying rural areas and moved inside the city proper. These were praised by those who wanted to stay outside the city. They were willing to acknowledge the good work but were not willing to follow.

This reluctance caused the leaders to form a plan to populate the city in a compulsory way. They cast lots so that each tribe was equally required to send one out of every ten families to live in the city. The city was populated and could function, but not as well as it could had the people joyfully volunteered.

Not many are willing to give up their personal comfort for the good of the kingdom of God, even among professing Christians. It would be good if each of us was more like those who voluntarily moved to the city. Their example shows us that it is better to give up personal comfort for the benefit of the kingdom and the glory of God.

We should examine ourselves and make sure we are not just cheering for those who dedicate themselves to God. We need to be following their example!

Build your wall...

- Do others have to encourage you to worship or are you the one encouraging others?

- Should we threaten people with eternal condemnation if they will not come to church when we invite them?

- Can you name any (even just one) personal comfort or convenience that you have given up in your service to God?

47 • Former Glory

"Now these are the chief of the province that dwelt in Jerusalem: but in the cities of Judah dwelt every one in his possession in their cities, to wit, Israel, the priests, and the Levites, and the Nethinims, and the children of Solomon's servants." – Nehemiah 11:3

Today, I would like to focus on a single verse. Actually, I want to focus on a single word: *province.*

Look how David described the city of Jerusalem and its majesty.

"Beautiful for situation, the joy of the whole earth, is mount Zion, on the sides of the north, the city of the great King." – Psalm 48:2

The once great city of Zion and kingdom of Israel is now reduced to a *province* of Persia. Because of Israel's disobedience, the people were in bondage several times. The Lord delivered them out of their bondage each time but there were lasting consequences from their sins. One of those effects was that Israel would never return to her former glory as David described.

It is by our choices that we determine whether we will live day to day in the glory of the kingdom or as a shadow of the good blessings that once were. The quality of our church life lies not only in the hands of the pastor but ALL the members of the local church.

If we only partly devote ourselves to God and His church, we should expect no more than the experience of living in an insignificant province. However, if the church body unites in deep devotion to God and one another, they will reap the joys of living in the glorious kingdom of the gospel church!

Please read Nehemiah 11:4-36

Previously, I mentioned that we will only experience the glory of God in our worship to the extent which we give ourselves in devotion to Him. This article will show a few of the ways we can become a lively body of Christ.

The remaining verses of Chapter 11 give details of the responsibilities of each family in the city of Jerusalem. There were gatherers of wood or water, handymen for repairs, singers to announce sacrifices, those who led prayers, and others who taught the word of God. There were many duties required to keep the city operating and support worship in the temple.

There are many things to do in the church today as well. Not everyone is going to be a preacher or a song leader. God has given His children many gifts to benefit the church. Rather than waiting for someone to assign us a job, we should seek how we can benefit our local church in ways large and small.

- Is there a member who is home bound? Go visit them.
- Is there someone who wants to come to church but cannot get themselves there? Go get them.
- Are there repairs that need to be made to the church house or a member's home? Pick up a hammer and fix it.
- Is there someone sick or struggling with a sin? Pray for them. Visit them. Counsel them.
- Is there someone in financial trouble? Give to them generously.

Needless to say, there are plenty of things to do in the church, not just these I have listed.

You will notice that all of these services are for the benefit of others not for our own personal glory. Being devoted to God means that we are devoted to our brothers and sisters in Christ. The Bible teaches that our gifts of ministry are for the benefit of our home church.

> *"And he gave some, apostles; and some, prophets; and some, evangelists; and some, pastors and teachers; For the perfecting of the saints, for the work of the ministry, for the edifying of the body of Christ: Till we all come in the unity of the faith, and of the knowledge of the Son of God, unto a perfect man, unto the measure of the stature of the fulness of Christ:" – Ephesians 4:11-13*

God has chosen you to Himself, and He has called you into the service of His kingdom. The focus of every believer should be to glorify God by helping others in the church until The Lord returns.

> *"And let us not be weary in well doing: for in due season we shall reap, if we faint not. As we have therefore opportunity, let us do good unto all men, especially unto them who are of the household of faith."*
> *– Galatians 6:9-10*

Build your wall...

- What should we do if we feel that church is no longer as joyful as it was before?

- Does past blessing in a church guarantee future blessing?

48 • Are You Thankful for the Ministers of God?

Please read Nehemiah 12:1-26

This portion of Nehemiah gives a rather lengthy list of the priests, Levites, and other religious leaders through several generations. We do not know much about most of those in this list. However, the inclusion of such a list does teach us a valuable lesson regarding those who minister the word of God to the people.

We owe a huge debt of gratitude to those faithful ministers who, with the Lord's help, started the church where we meet each Sunday. We are not to revere them as gods, but we should learn about them and hold them in high regard for their work.

We owe our utmost respect and support to our current pastors and ministers. They care for us in so many ways. They pray for us, admonish us, teach us, and motivate us. Consider the following:

> *"Obey them that have the rule over you, and submit yourselves: for they watch for your souls, as they that must give account, that they may do it with joy, and not with grief: for that is unprofitable for you." –*
> *Hebrews 13:17*

The care of the flock of God has been given to these men. They answer to God for our instruction and correction. It would be good for us to make it a little easier on them.

> *"Let the elders that rule well be counted worthy of double honour, especially they who labour in the word and doctrine."*
>
> *– 1st Timothy 5:17*

This honor includes both respect to their word and position as well as financial support. If at all possible, we should support our ministry so that they are not torn between a secular job and Bible study and prayer.

Additionally, we ought to rejoice when a young man shows signs of a calling to the gospel ministry. It should give us great hope that the Lord will continue to shine a light in our community through our church when we have passed on. Support these young men with prayer and study in the word.

Build your wall...

⚒ What can you do to support your pastor more?

⚒ When is the last time you did something to encourage your pastor? What did you do?

49 • Dedicate Everything to God

Please read Nehemiah 12:27-47

This portion of scripture tells the story of the great day of celebration when Israel dedicated the wall of Jerusalem. This dedication was not a celebration of themselves or their personal accomplishments. It was an acknowledgement that God had brought them thus far and that they would continue to put their trust in Him.

While I do not believe that dedication ceremonies are called for in the case of our homes or meeting houses, I do believe we should make it clear that these places are dedicated for the worship of God. Then, we should behave in them accordingly.

In our homes, we should realize that all that we have is a blessing from God. As a family, we should live holy and righteous to the best of our ability. We should make Godly decisions with our finances, entertainment, and education of not only our children but the parents as well. We should also make it clear, by our behavior, that we expect any guest in our home to honor God with their words and deeds.

Our meeting houses should be houses of worship. Whether we are meeting in formal worship, Bible study, a meal, or for fellowship we must remember that we exist to glorify God. Our minds should be humble and grateful every time we enter the building, and we should be filled with joy that we are blessed to have a safe meeting house.

Our houses of worship should receive at least as much care and upkeep as our personal homes. An ornate structure is not necessary, and could possibly be distracting. But a well-kept structure and grounds show thankfulness to God for the gift of the meeting house.

This dedication can easily be embodied in our homes and houses of worship, but it goes much further than that. These verses in Nehemiah end with the reaction of the people to the proclaimed dedication. They respond with work and worship toward God. Likewise, we should dedicate our lives to God and then LIVE IT!

I recall the words of the hymn writer Isaac Watts:

> *"Thus far the Lord hath led me on,*
> *Thus far His power prolongs my days,*
> *And every evening shall make known*
> *Some fresh memorial of His grace."*

Build your wall...

- What can we do to make sure others understand that our household (house) is dedicated to the worship of God?

- Is it wrong to have non-worship activities in our church house? Explain.

50 • It's Not About You (or Me)!

Please read Nehemiah 13:1-14

A few years ago, I was casually walking through a Christian bookstore and a title caught my eye. I do not remember the exact title, but it was something like "What Have We Done?" It had a cover picture of people playing electric guitars and a crowd jumping up and down. I was kind of curious why such a book would be in this kind of store, so I picked it up and read a little.

The main purpose of the book was to show what a huge mistake it was to bring in modern rock music to a worship service. This was not someone, like me, observing from the outside. This was a man who had once encouraged the idea in order to draw in a younger, hipper crowd. His conclusion? They got a younger, hipper crowd that really wanted nothing to do with the word of God or righteous living. They just liked the rock music.

As we have already seen in the book of Nehemiah, the physical events of the Old Testament have spiritual application for us today.

In response to the law of God, the Israelites separated themselves from the nations around them. In fact, when Nehemiah returned and saw that Eliashib was still making deals with Tobiah, he aggressively removed Tobiah, his things, and his influence!

They stopped acting like their worldly neighbors, and began seeking righteous living. The Israelites did not allow the world or its practices in their Biblical worship.

Christians today should look, act, and speak differently than the sinful world. Our homes, as we have already discussed, should be dedicated to God. Our houses of worship should be set apart as well. We should not use the things of the world in worship because the things of this world attract *worldly* people who do not fear God nor seek righteousness.

This is not to discourage evangelism in the world. We are to go everywhere preaching (and living) the gospel. The simple approach of sharing the word through preaching or Bible study worked for the first century church.

Why do we now feel that we need tricks and shows to draw in the people? Is the gospel no longer sufficient?

I saw a cartoon clip one time that had a younger and older lady walking together out of a church meeting. The young lady said, "You know, I just didn't get much out of today's service." The older lady responded, "That's good. It wasn't about you!"

Church is not about us and our personal preferences. It is about God.

Build your wall...

- What is the difference between an aid to worship and an addition to worship?

- If your church was forced to hide in secret and not meet in the church house, would it survive?

51 • Keep the Lord's Day Holy

Please read Nehemiah 13:15-22

The Sabbath was created by God for man. Jesus confirms this in Mark 2:27:

> *"And he said unto them, The sabbath was made for man, and not man for the sabbath:"*

It was designed as a day of rest from work. It was also designed as a day to focus on the Lord and His worship. This observance is so important that God included it in His top ten list!

> *"Remember the sabbath day, to keep it holy." – Exodus 20:8*

There are some today that feel it is no longer important to observe this commandment. I have heard that, when Jesus declared that He was Lord of the Sabbath, we were set free from its observance. The problem with this argument is that Jesus is God. He observed the first sabbath after creation, and He and the Father have been working ever since.

> *"My Father worketh hitherto, and I work." – John 5:17*

The point Jesus was making during His earthly ministry was that the observance of the Sabbath should not be used to lord over the children of God like the Pharisees. We are to worship and rest from our secular jobs, but we are to still do good things on the Sabbath, especially, if it involves showing love and compassion for another person.

There is also another debate about when this should be observed. In the Old Testament, Saturday was the Sabbath. However, it is *very* clear from scripture that immediately after Christ's resurrection, on the first day of the week, there was a shift in the day of worship to the Lord's Day, which is Sunday.

> *"Now when Jesus was risen early the first day of the week, he appeared first to Mary Magdalene, out of whom he had cast seven devils." –* *Mark 16:9*

He rose on a Sunday, and He came to visit His disciples on Sundays.

> *"Then the same day at evening, being the first day of the week, when the doors were shut where the disciples were assembled for fear of the Jews, came Jesus and stood in the midst, and saith unto them, Peace be unto you." – John 20:19*

> *"And after eight days again his disciples were within, and Thomas with them: then came Jesus, the doors being shut, and stood in the midst, and said, Peace be unto you." – John 20:26*

We then see that this continues into the time of the ministry of Paul.

> *"And upon the first day of the week, when the disciples came together to break bread, Paul preached unto them, ready to depart on the morrow; and continued his speech until midnight." – Acts 20:7*

The pattern continues on in Revelation, Chapter 1 where we find John on the Isle of Patmos worshipping on the Lord's day, which is Sunday. Therefore, we *should* continue to observe a sabbath, and it should be on Sunday. It is proper to cease from our earthly labors for a day and focus on the worship of God. We would also do well if we cease from doing business on that day so others may observe the day of rest and worship as well.

Build your wall...

Is it OK to substitute Sunday worship by attending a service Saturday evening? Explain.

What kinds of activities could you do on Sunday that are not formal worship but still honoring to God?

52 • Choose Your Friends Wisely

"In those days also saw I Jews that had married wives of Ashdod, of Ammon, and of Moab: and their children spake half in the speech of Ashdod, and could not speak in the Jews' language, but according to the language of each people. And I contended with them, and cursed them, and smote certain of them, and plucked off their hair, and made them swear by God, saying, Ye shall not give your daughters unto their sons, nor take their daughters unto your sons, or for yourselves. Did not Solomon king of Israel sin by these things? yet among many nations was there no king like him, who was beloved of his God, and God made him king over all Israel: nevertheless even him did outlandish women cause to sin. Shall we then hearken unto you to do all this great evil, to transgress against our God in marrying strange wives? And one of the sons of Joiada, the son of Eliashib the high priest, was son in law to Sanballat the Horonite: therefore I chased him from me. Remember them, O my God, because they have defiled the priesthood, and the covenant of the priesthood, and of the Levites. Thus cleansed I them from all strangers, and appointed the wards of the priests and the Levites, every one in his business; and for the wood offering, at times appointed, and for the firstfruits. Remember me, O my God, for good."
– Nehemiah 13:23-31.

I find it *very* interesting that among the last things mentioned in the reforms Nehemiah records is that of mixed marriages with the pagan cultures around Israel. Perhaps it is because this is the devil's best tool for drawing the children of God away from their righteous walk! This admonition talks about marriage, but it can be applied to all relationships.

Among those that Nehemiah mentions who were brought down by evil spouses was Solomon. Other than the Lord Jesus, Solomon was probably the wisest man that ever walked the face of the earth! If he was led away by bad relationships and keeping the wrong friends, why should we think we would do better?

Paul instructs quite clearly,

> *"Be not deceived: evil communications corrupt good manners." – 1st Corinthians 15:33*

This is not to say that we should not try to help those in sin to overcome it. However, the general trend through history has proven that if we hang out with evil people, we start acting like them rather than the other way around.

Fellowship is vital to our devotion to God. John says,

> *"And this commandment have we from him, That he who loveth God love his brother also." – 1st John 4:21*

But we should choose our friends wisely! We should surround ourselves with other godly people seeking righteousness. If we only fellowship with the Lord's people for a few moments on Sunday, we are going to be fighting a losing battle against the world's influence on us.

Nehemiah then ends his account by asking God to remember him for good. Nehemiah was strengthened by the power of God to do great things. He obeyed the Spirit moving in him and did the great things God had called him to do. When the work was finished, he thanked the Lord and begged for the favor of God in his life that God promised to those who would follow Him.

How often do we pray this way? I find I am asking forgiveness more often than anything else. The story of Nehemiah should remind us there is a more abundant life for us in God's kingdom here. God has promised to bless those that follow Him. When we do, we do not deserve the blessings of God for our obedience. But, God has promised it.

Remember what we have learned. God is merciful and ready to forgive. He also delights in blessing His children. Consider these words from James as we end this survey of the book of Nehemiah.

> *"Be afflicted, and mourn, and weep: let your laughter be turned to mourning, and your joy to heaviness. Humble yourselves in the sight of the Lord, and he shall lift you up." – James 4:9-10*

He SHALL lift you up!

Build your wall…

- Name your friends or regular influences and the kinds of things they like to do.

- Do you surround yourself with people that encourage Godly living or just those who you like or share a common interest?

Dear Reader,

I hope that this little book has been of some benefit to you, your family, and your church. Most of all, I pray that God has been glorified in the writing of this book, and in your rebuilding of your life in His service. If I have said anything contrary to the word of God, please forgive me, pray for me, and let me know your thoughts. I only seek to worship the Lord in spirit and in truth.

If this book has been of benefit to you, please consider sharing it with others.

May the Lord bless you is my prayer.

Your little brother,

Bryce

www.ingramcontent.com/pod-product-compliance
Lightning Source LLC
Chambersburg PA
CBHW022054050726
47591CB00002B/530